THE VIRGIN WEIRD
INTERNET GUIDE

THE VIRGIN WEIRD INTERNET GUIDE

VERSION 1.0

Steve Hornby

This edition first published in 2000 by
Virgin Publishing Ltd
Thames Wharf Studios
Rainville Road
London W6 9HA

Version 1.0 – November 2000

Reprinted 2000

A catalogue record for this book is available from the British Library.

ISBN 0 7535 0449 9

Typeset by Galleon Typesetting, Ipswich

Printed and bound by Omnia Books Ltd, Glasgow

//HOW WOULD YOU LIKE TO SKIVE TODAY?

The Internet is the cheapest ever method of publishing. It means that you need only a modicum of talent for your musings, ideas and ravings to be read in every country at very little or no cost. As a result, just about every crackpot idea under the sun has somehow made it on to a website. From the earliest days, nerds, geeks and eccentrics started raising the stakes for the trophy of 'the world's weirdest website'.

As the Internet penetrated office life, the humble PC was promoted from glorified typewriter to powerful communications device. Email stopped the boss telling you off for all those personal phone calls and a whole culture of surreptitious office skiving was born. While everyone – from directors to secretaries – is staring diligently at their computer screens, they're probably checking up on sports results or marvelling at a webcam beaming out of some bar somewhere. Today, emails containing addresses and links for daft websites fly around the world's offices at incredible speeds, making global celebrities out of humble site owners.

The web is notorious for many different things: news, shopping, freaks and pornography. But one of the best things about it is the glimpse it gives into the stranger and wilder outposts of the human imagination, via sites made for no financial gain – they exist simply because they *can*. This book is a celebration of the Internet heroes who have put the hilarious ideas that previously only ever existed in drunken moments straight into the limelight. The following pages contain links to some of the daftest websites that have ever made it on to the World Wide Web. Long may they, and their kind, continue.

The future for the World Weird Web is looking bright. It's getting easier to produce polished, professional-looking web pages and cheaper to register your own domain names. So the silly sites of the past will still be around – but they'll look a lot more professional than they used to. And there's a new development just around the corner: with digital technology becoming cheaper by the day, filmmakers and animators are finding that they don't have to tow the corporate line any more. They can distribute their cracked visions over the web without being constrained by men in suits. With broadband Internet access (with its near-broadcast-quality video) about to break, conventional TV scheduling and channels could well become a thing of the past, with people being able to watch what they like when they like. A good laugh will only ever be a few clicks away.

Steve Hornby was charged by *Empire* magazine to plumb the depths of human stupidity and uncover the most bonkers ideas on the web for his notorious column, *Dr Steve's Internet Clinic*. He's eternally grateful to everyone who bombarded him with all types of web-based nonsense to fill the pages of this book, while he should have been knuckling down to some hard work in his real job of pushing back the boundaries of interactive media.

It's much more difficult to keep track of weird websites than of sensible ones. They don't belong to big companies and are put together by a ragged bunch of individuals, so they can change servers (and addresses) often. If any of the sites are mysteriously gone when you type in the address, don't assume they no longer exist: just go to your favourite search engine and type in the name of the site. If the site really has been killed off or you find a loony site that you think should be in this book, please let us know by emailing us at **response@virgin-pub.co.uk**. We'll make sure it's dealt with in the next edition.

//CONTENTS

1//THE INTERNET AND THE MODERN WORLD

It's fair to say that in the last five years the Internet has changed beyond recognition. Slowly it's been changing the world around us as people's insatiable urge to communicate sucks up more and more bandwidth. Email is undoubtedly the Internet's 'killer app' and it's inconceivable to think of working for a large corporation where email isn't the primary method of communication. Just as these same individuals take it for granted that they can surf the web from their desktop PCs when they think nobody's watching. In fact, such is the popularity of the web that it's now possible to use it to educate yourself, buy just about anything that you need and, if you really put your mind to it, find all your entertainment.

In the space of the last few years it's become accepted that every major company has its own website to allow people to find its offices, shout about what it does and even sell its products. These are generally complicated websites containing hundreds of pages of information stored in complex databases producing intricately designed pages. The company brand is pushed around the clock while being meticulously maintained with the most up-to-date information by teams of dedicated specialists.

It hasn't always been that way, though. Ten years ago websites were bizarre affairs with crude text links and grey pages that had been seen only by people who worked in government departments or academia. The web, or, more specifically, the computer code it was written in, HTML (hypertext mark-up language), was seen as a simple method of publishing archives of text with the occasional picture. These text archives could be accessed in a very different way from traditional linear methods – such as reading a book cover to cover. Certain words in a paragraph of text could be hyperlinked to another page, so in a scientific document a word or technical term could be explained in more detail on a separate page, without disturbing the flow of the main text. This allowed a more personalised interactive experience in which the users could follow their own path through the pages, taking in only as much as they wanted.

More and more of these pages emerged on a baffling number of sites. Finding them became a problem, and so search engines were invented. Initially, they were like phone books compiled by reviewers, who meticulously catalogued websites and their contents. Then, when someone remembered that they were all hosted on machines capable of performing powerful calculations and were not written on pieces of paper, websites became searchable, so that a keyword entry would throw up links to a number of different sites. Ultimately, the reviewers have been ditched and banks of computers endlessly search and catalogue the web so that, next time someone wants to know about, say, green wellies, they'll be greeted with a baffling array of possibilities.

Trying To Make the World a Better Place

When the web was the sole preserve of academia and government, before corporations discovered it, website content was broadly divided into two types. The first and major use was as a cheap and cheerful method of publishing information and sharing ideas. No longer would obscure scientific magazines with a print run of fifty copies have to go bust because interested parties had no idea where to get hold of them – or that they even existed. The whole thing could be published on the web with practically no production costs, and readers could all interact with each other through Usenet news groups. Great scientific minds could get together and help each other out with their problems; scientific advances would be an everyday occurrence; disease and poverty would disappear; and the world would be a better place.

Students

The other use of the web was by university students who were traditionally allocated webspace on their college servers. Most didn't care and ignored this fact, but the types of students who were interested in publishing their own newspapers or were mildly interested in computers suddenly found that they had a global, if slightly limited, voice. The majority of these websites were dismal efforts that would never interest anyone except the people responsible for them. They were of the 'Hello, everyone, look at me!' ilk, which tended to list that person's painfully mundane interests and pastimes. The more gifted students suddenly realised that they'd been given the key to open a door to the world. HTML was, and almost still is, no more difficult to code than using an early word processor. Not since the advent of the printing press had the automation of the dissemination of knowledge and ideas been so simple, and now completely cost free. It wasn't surprising to find that the content of these early student websites could be as mundane and pointless as the individuals themselves talking of their radical opinions, angst-ridden sentiments, heroic tales of drinking and so forth. Sometimes, the odd gem could be found.

As Internet-enabled PCs broke out of the halls of academia into the corridors of corporate institutions, the web effectively broke cover and went 'overground' in the US. Before long, there was actually enough stuff on the web for people to want to start accessing it from home, and so Internet Service Providers (ISPs) popped up to give people access without their having to pay corporate prices. What really sent Internet usage soaring was the fact that the local calls in the US were free.

The Global Scrapbook

When emails became a way of life in the States, the Internet soon took off. ISPs and, more importantly, companies such as Geocities started offering web hosting for free. Now with a modicum of

HTML aptitude it was possible to put together a website and fire it off to the hosting company for all the world to see.

For thousands of people it was like having their scrapbooks, photo albums and fanzines on a global platform. Obviously, the content of these sites wasn't as important as being able to say that you had one of your own. Thoughts, obsessions, interests, hobbies and embarrassing photos are being uploaded to the web every day. It's becoming a repository for the population's thoughts.

Just as the first press industrialised the printing of books, freeing monks to do monklike things, so the web is changing the way people receive their information. Bearing in mind that most people, unlike in medieval times, can actually read and even compose their own sentences, the web has shown the fastest growth of any medium of communication in history.

Pub gigs have traditionally been patrolled by fanzine authors pedalling their wares, having sneakily used their parents' photocopiers to print out their masterpieces. But the Internet changed that. You didn't even have to own a computer: everyone knew someone with access to the Internet. Suddenly fanzines rocketed out of crusty pubs on to a global platform as the electronic magazine, or ezine, was born. With absolutely no quality controls whatsoever, ezines are a pretty hit-or-miss affair. Subject matter ranges from music scenes, through films, to almost unhealthy obsessions with certain actresses.

Censorship and the Web
While the Internet does allow a certain amount of speech, it is inevitably at the forefront of attacks from groups who are threatened by *freedom* of speech.

Only a fool would deny that there is a lot of unpalatable content on the web – fascism, pornography and the like – but it is such a minute proportion of what is out there that the calls to ban the

Internet seem to have missed the point. There's a lot of pornography in bookshops and newsagents, too, but not many people in the developed world have been burning books recently, and it's inconceivable to think that newsagents should be banned.

Every child-molesting serial killer who's convicted of horrific crimes from now on will be analysed and be found to have used the Internet in the past and been obsessed with activities that are plainly illegal and utterly immoral. It's interesting to know that, in a recent survey of convicted murderers on Death Row in US jails, the majority of them cited *To Kill A Mockingbird* as their favourite book. It's not that the Internet invented or even caused these people to do horrible things: it just made their getting hold of this type of material that much easier. Dodgy old men have been selling pornographic and snuff material under the counter in book and video stores for years and the furore about video had all but died down when the web reared its ugly child-molesting face. The debate will rage on.

What's It All For, Then?
The web is a fantastic resource for finding information but, more interestingly, there's a lot of funny stuff out there. Strangely, now that owning your own funny site doesn't seem to be such a novelty any more – unless you're going to try to make some money out of it – the number of ridiculous splurge-of-consciousness websites seems to be dwindling.

This guide attempts to be the cream of the crop of ridiculous ideas that have been committed to HTML. Bearing in mind that students inevitably get turfed out of college at some point and people swap ISPs with great frequency, it's likely that a lot of these sites listed won't be there any more. The chances are, though, that they're still on the web, but at a different address. So, if they're gone or typing in some of the horrific addresses for these sites seems a bit daunting, the best thing to do, as we said earlier, is haul up your favourite search engine and find them that way.

2//ADVERTISING

The advertising industry took to the web like a duck to water. No messy printing or expensive film shoots: just hire an agency and start creaming in the client's money.

Absurd Gallery   http://absurdgallery.com
A collection of bizarre but real ads, labels and signs – marvel at the audacity of lard ads and Jenny McCarthy farting to sell shoes.

Adbusters   www.adbusters.org
If you're one of those people who find themselves screaming at the TV screen when advertisers use their favourite tunes to sell some piece of household rubbish, then Adbusters is your first port of call to get even. A genuine organisation whose sole purpose is to reclaim popular culture from the evil clutches of corporate marketing types through spoof adverts and TV uncommercials.

AdCritic   www.adcritic.com
AdCritic.com was created for those who find advertising more than just an annoyance between TV shows but delight in it and probably earn a hefty living from it. Anyone can be an armchair critic but this site is really for professionals who upload, dissect and analyse ads from all over the world.

The Big Sell Out   www2.gol.com/users/ian/shamepics
A collection of the photos that today's celebrities would probably not like to be reminded of. All actors go through lean patches 'between jobs' and it seems that quite a few of them sneaked off to foreign climes to advertise household products safe in the knowledge that their US fan base would never see them demean themselves. Or so they thought. Find out how Bruce Willis, Sly, Arnie, Harrison Ford, Madonna and even Quentin Tarantino paid their mortgages during those dark times.

Clawde the Lobster
www.redlobster.com/escape/clawde.htm

If the sight of a 25-foot-long, 11-foot-high and 8-foot-wide lobster bolted on a white pickup truck has just convinced you that you've lost your mind, don't worry. You've just met Clawde the Lobster, the advertising 'spokes-gimmick' for a seafood restaurant chain.

eNormicom!
www.enormicom.com

eNormicom are the ad agency that will transform your tiny business to a multinational corporation within minutes. Well, possibly, but with hyperbole worthy of Muhammed Ali this spoof company has probably lured its fair share of suckers. Particularly close to the mark is the eNormicom Image Bucket Program, which is claimed to help companies with an e-dentity crisis.

Junk Busters
www.junkbusters.com

Fight off the invasion of marketers. If you're sick of junk mail, banner ads or cold calling then fight back with the handy little tips listed here.

Mascot Orphanage
www.lileks.com/institute/orphanage

More like a mascot old folk's home, this is where they're concealed when they're past their sell-buy date to be ignored and abused. The halls are teeming with the likes of 'Kraut King', 'Mr Heating', 'Radiant Roast', 'Happy Egg' and 'Bondex Betty', who are looking for a website to adopt them. Each one even comes complete with its own biography.

The New Yorker Inane Ad of the Week
www.2street.com/newyorker

Poking fun at the Big Apple's chattering classes, this site claims to highlight 'an especially absurd advertisement from the pages of the militantly bourgeois *New Yorker* magazine'. Positively seething with hatred for this affluent portion of the market who delight in spending money on things that they didn't even know that they wanted until they were told by a magazine.

The Pit of Advertising Wonders

www.kkcltd.com/
pit4/jingle.html

Ad execs are the media version of estate agents – of dubious point with an overinflated vision of their own self-importance. Making itself look even more ridiculous than it really is, one ad agency has set up this little connection. A truly despicable effort that allows the poor unfortunates who couldn't make it into the world of washing-powder commercials a taste of what they're missing. There's a chance to write jingles and straplines for fictitious products but no opportunity to get drunk and obnoxious in wine bars at lunchtime, boring the pants off everyone within earshot by regaling tales into your mobile phone of your last successful pitch at full volume.

Potato in a Box

http://welcome.to/potatoinabox

Spoof ad for a truly uninspiring instant meal. Each individually packaged spud comes with its own free sachet of mud.

3//ANIMALS

The feline of the species and other household pets

There's a widely held belief that people who prefer cats to dogs are generally more introverted, shy, artistic and prone to eccentricity. Coincidentally this also seems to be a reasonable description of the kind of people who really get off on computers. Perhaps this is a potential explanation for the proliferation of feline-themed sites cluttering up the web. Dog owners, on the other hand, are smug in the knowledge that their pets are fundamentally dumb creatures that couldn't and wouldn't want to survive without them. Their cat-owning counterparts rejoice in the exact opposite and, maybe because little Tiddles is so self-contained, they're always imagining he's displaying human behavioural characteristics. When they think they've found them, boy, are they pleased with themselves! And they just want to share them with the world. In the old days it just used to be boring the pants off anyone unfortunate enough to come across their path. Now they've got a global platform and there are plenty of like-minded individuals who are just delighted to share their delusions. Alternatively, there are other types of domestic pets.

The Bad Iguana List   **www.geocities.com/bad_pets/ BadPets/BadIguana.html**

A treasury of iguana misdemeanours that keeps growing. Reptile owners are asked to submit things that their pets have destroyed, attempted to eat and urinated on. Highly amusing and presumably doing the rounds of the office email circuit.

Barnaby the Ferret   **www.barnaby.loveslife.com**

Anyone remiss enough to have cancelled their subscription to *Modern Ferret* magazine will be a stranger to the charms of this furry fan bag.

Bearded   www.littlewilderness.com/
Dragons   bearded_dragons.htm
Fifty-foot-high, fire-breathing terror. Well actually a spectacularly ugly type of lizard and quite a lot smaller. All the procurement and maintenance needs are catered for here.

Bunny Goes Raving   www.undergroundlondon.com/bunny
Cutesy little bunny does it large in this interactive comic strip.

The Canine Café!   www.k9treat.com
The only place to be seen for today's pampered pooches. Barbara's Canine Catering and Dog Bakery offers an eat-in or delivery service for the next time your hound decides to throw a party. The service is so complete that even ultra-sensitive dogs with allergies are looked after.

The Cat That Looks   www.homeroom1.com/
Like Hitler   history.html
Check out Pete, the world's only feline fascist. The fact that most white cats can look like this with just a dab from a Magic Marker does call into question the authenticity of the site. Strangely enough, his owner is quite proud of him.

Easter Bunny Hunters of America   www.wsu.edu/~twl/bunny
One of the most coveted hunting prizes. Apparently, their fur is of the highest quality and is great for coats and even makes good toilet-seat covers. Extreme sport for the fearless hunter.

The Flying   www.mediafarm.no/
Cow   forsoksgard/kukaster.asp
Virtual animal abuse. If you've ever been prevented from flinging a full-grown cow across a field with a catapult and were too hampered by morals, then this is the place. Use skill to hurl the hapless bovine into the next world.

How to Wash a Cat   **www.justsaywow.com/cat.htm**

Cats are about as hydrophobic as any animal without rabies is likely to get. So the twisted creature that devised this site is probably just trying to upset the world's cat owners. Worryingly, the first bit of advice is to 'thoroughly clean the toilet'. No surprise to discover that the next thing to do is stuff moggy down the porcelain and give it a good flush. Wait for a knock on the door from the RSPCA.

Internet   **www.execpc.com/~judyheim/**
For Cats   **Internet4cats.html**

This is such a hit that it's spun off a book, *Internet for Cats: A Guide to How You and Your Cat Can Prowl the Information Highway Together*. Rammed with all the predictable jokes about taming your mouse and a guide to Kitty Netiquette, this is all you need to enjoy a night in with your cat and your PC. Alternatively borrow a dog and at least you'll get out of the house a bit more.

Leeches USA   **www.assileeches.com**

Are they tools of medieval quackery or miracles of the modern medical world? Leeches are strange creatures with some very weird mythology. Find out the truth about these blood-sucking slugs here.

A Patent for Entertaining a Cat   **www.patents.ibm.com/cgi-bin/**
Using a Laser Pointer   **viewpat.cmd/US05443036__**

The ultimate accolade for mad inventor types is to get their latest project patented – although the person who bought a laser pointer and tormented his cat with it is hardly in line for a Nobel Prize. Still, it may be a good way of running a few pounds off an overweight puss.

Strange Foreign Objects   **www.watchingyou.com/**
in Dog Faeces   **poop.html**

To the owner of this site – desperate for his own unique offering but suffering from a lack of creative inspiration – it came like a bolt out of the blue when he was out walking his dog. Hard at work with his pooper scooper, he noticed that his dog had eaten and passed some missing jewellery. He took his research a little further and – hey presto! – he got a truly unique idea to showcase his eccentricities.

The Swine Enthusiast   **www.swine-enthusiast.com**
No it's not illegal, just a place where people who like pigs get together.

Tarantula Planet   **www.tarantulaplanet.org**
Little boys who really want to scare little girls need to choose the right weapon. This is the lifestyle guide for the ultimate creepy-crawly. With screensavers and postcards.

Toilet-Train   **www.rainfrog.com/**
Your Cat   **mishacat/toilet.shtml**
Misha is a well-trained cat, it seems – so well mannered, in fact, that the owner of said feline has decided to share toilet-training secrets with web surfers the world over. 'How To Toilet Train Your Cat' is a site dedicated to making sure you never have to clean your carpet of an unsightly mess ever again. HTTTYC is packed with detailed instructions and photos illustrating how your moggy should use a domestic WC.

Tony & Charlotte's   **www.woodbat.co.uk/**
Stick-Insect Page   **stick.htm**
For truly on-the-wall fun for the pet owner who just has to be different. This couple are just dying to share their unique house guests with the world.

Twisty   **www.etexweb.com/personal/**
Cats   **speir/twisty/twisty.htm**
GM foods can't hold a candle to cats that behave like kangaroos. These little insults to nature go by the name of Twisty Cats. If there's a feline equivalent of the Kennel Club then one glance at their owners' antics should have them drummed out quick smart.

Unofficial Mr Bigglesworth Fan Club

http://welcome.to/ MrBigglesworthFanClub

The lap ornament of the Dr Evil, Austin Powers' nemesis, not only has his own fan club but he was voted 'Cat of the Year' by *Cats* magazine. This page contains everything there is to know about this bizarre-looking bald feline: press cuttings, sound bites and photos. Better join the fan club, because it says, 'When Mr Bigglesworth gets upset people die.' You have been warned.

Why Cats Paint

www.monpa.com

Cat sceptics, convinced that moggies are semi-feral animals whose sole medium of expressing affection is depositing half-eaten birds on doorsteps, think again. Why do they do it? Probably because their mad owners make them. Try telling your friends that little Tiddles is Leonardo da Vinci and they'll probably try to have you committed.

You Know You're a Guinea Pig Slave When . . .

www.geocities.com/Heartland/ Plains/2517/slave.html

You make a web page out of it? That's a sure sign.

Wild animals

It's not just domestic animals that amuse. There's plenty of hilarity out in the wild.

The Bone Voyage Travel Case

http://home.earthlink.net/ ~mnmprd

There's no reason why pooches can't be as stylish as their owners when they travel. The Bone Voyage travel case will look good parked next to matching Samsonites. It even comes with containers for food and water, a shampoo bottle, a flea-spray bottle, a flea comb and extra space for medicines.

Cow Tipping Disgraceland Style
www.nwlink.com/~timelvis/cowtip.html

Learn how to master this ultimate drunken student prank. Practise virtual 'tipping' on 'Cud Elvis, the King of Rock'n'Roll' bovines and discover seventeen ways of making a cow go insane. It's cruel, but if your vegetarian conscience gets the better of you then there's always the section on Things to Do in Tulsa Other than Cow Tipping.

The Cow Liberation Front
http://lehrerz1.rz.uni-karlsruhe.de/~za276/zeitung/england/cow6.htm

Right on, kids! The web is a hotbed of animal activism, at its forefront the Cow Liberation Front, freeing bovines of their shackles – well, rings through their noses at least. Join the campaign, or for the less socially aware just download the wet-nosed, cud-chewing fellas.

Cows With Guns
www.cowswithguns.com/homepage.html

That whole farming thing is deeply entrenched in the Kiwi culture. Even when they escape to the heady world of rock'n'roll they can't let it drop. This is a bovine-themed band that has made it big on the American indie circuit.

Fenton, the Death Sheep From Hell
www.deathsheep.com

Think twice about sheep being woolly morons destined to end up skewered as a kebab. Fenton is a truly evil creature who's spreading his violence and hatred through this website to establish his ewe world order. Can be viewed in sheepish.

Headlice
www.headlice.org

It's one of the great ironies of life that it's always the posh kids at school that end up infested and scratching themselves to the bone. To find out just about everything that's ever been found out about these nasty little pests check out the official home of headlice.

Ichthyology Division of   **www.flmnh.ufl.edu/**
Florida University   **fish/default.htm**

One viewing of *Jaws* is enough to give most people a shark phobia. Not the people in this university department, though: they're going to make a career out of them. Lots of fascinating shark-related information, including details of the daddy of them all, the megamouth shark.

The Infamous Exploding   **www.perp.com/whale/**
Whale   **video.html**

Real-life footage of the detonation of a 45-foot, eight-ton, dead whale that washed up on a beach in Oregon a few years ago. Unfamiliar with the proper disposal techniques, the local officials decided the best method was to fill it with dynamite and blast it to smithereens. Local film crews descended to capture the event for posterity and were deluged with decomposing whale meat. The videos live for ever on the web as a testament to man's stupidity.

The Naked Dancing Llama homepage   **www.frolic.org**

He wears absolutely no clothes, he rides a Harley Davidson and he's running for president. The NDL will provide the ignorant with pearls of wisdom and even personal advice. Well, llamas are intrinsically comedy animals put on Earth for our amusement and that's just what this site is all about.

Prawnography.net   **www.prawnography.net**

A site based on a simple pun. Warning that this website contains shellfish should be enough of a warning. It's designed and intended solely for organisms high enough in the food chain to appreciate the beauty of wanton marine life and hardcore crustaceans.

Scary Squirrel World   **www.scarysquirrel.org**

Squirrels – cute little scamps of cartoon legend or rats with bushy tails? A trip to Scary Squirrel World will stop the debate permanently and leave you spitting and hissing next time one sidles up to your picnic rug. The fact that they're responsible for road rage and the American Civil War will be news to most people, but visitors do get to join the renegade squirrel gang of their choice.

Seamonkey Worship page   users.uniserve.com/~sbarclay/ seamonk.htm

Those cute little underwater nuclear families so beloved of seventies comic ads are still around. Disappointment is still lurking for kids who open their packages to be greeted by a load of small shrimps. If this is your bag . . .

The Squashed Bug Zoo   http://squashed.roach.org/zoo.html

When heat waves and tourists seem like a distant memory, think of the one thing that encapsulates the summer. Sunshine? No – insect infestation. A healthy dose of nostalgia is provided by a visit to the Squashed Bug Zoo.

Squirrel Fishing   www.eecs.harvard.edu/~yaz/ en/squirrel_fishing.html

Just that they're cute shouldn't save them from becoming innocent playthings for man's pleasure. City types hard pressed to find a stretch of unpolluted water for a day's blood sports should take a trip to their local park. Indulge in squirrel fishing but don't tell your veggie buddies.

Turtle Foundation for World Domination   www.turtlegirl.com/ tffwd

Redressing the balance for our shelled friends by keeping them out of soup. Their day will come soon when they will rise, albeit very slowly.

4//ART & CULTURE

The defining characteristics of a nation can be seen in its art and culture. With the web being a global medium, it looks like the world is doomed.

Art

While a computer screen may not be the most enthralling medium for art, computers and, more importantly, the Internet are changing society. Artists are always going to have a thing or two to say about that. Whereas computer art hasn't seemed to develop beyond making some nice screens, artists are using their own websites to showcase their art to possibly more appreciative audiences and meeting other like-minded individuals. That's the theory, anyway. Potentially, what they're doing is showing the world that they're society's most eccentric individuals, inhabiting the very edges of the sanity envelope.

Art Cars   www.artcars.com

Italians are generally acknowledged as the masters of elevating the humble car from a mundane form of transport to a thing of beauty. Wrong! This website is entirely devoted to cars whose main function is to look, if not good, startling as opposed to merely moving from A to B. They're exhibited all over the world as moving artistic statements but can be seen together on this website.

ASCII Art Collection   www.chris.com/ascii

You have to be a *bona fide* computer nerd to really appreciate this. For those who don't even know what ASCII is, it's the simple alphabet and roman numerals and a few symbols. (OK, if you *really* want to know, it stands for American Standard Code for Information Interchange.) Using these to make art is really limiting the artist to a fairly small audience, although they'll probably email their delight to all their other nerd friends.

Bad Art www.badart.com

Lacking the highbrow aims of the Museum of Bad Art, this site aims to find the most appalling bad art and laugh at it. It's a collection of what barely passes as work from some of the least talented individuals ever to arm themselves with brushes. Exhibits include such masterpieces as *The Carousel Nun*, the bummer-trip *Eye-yi-yi* and the grotesquely sentimental *Orange Maiden*.

Bewitched.com www.bewitched.com

Redesign a stellar constellation in the style of Van Gogh's *The Starry Night*. Very clever but not very captivating. Computers take all the fun out of art because you can't snigger at the pretentious people trying to sound clever.

Brian Eno's Oblique www.nashville.net/~bryrock/
Strategies eno/oblique.html

Creative types who backed themselves into an inspiration cul-de-sac can seek help from top muso-intellectual ex-Roxy Music baldie Brian Eno. 'Mechanicalize Something Idiosyncratic' means present yourself with surreal dilemmas to jolt your brain back into action.

Bullseyeart www.bullseyeart.com/website

A collection of off-the-wall animations with titles such as *Internet: The Animated Series*, *The Rhino and Nutmeg Show*, *Miss Muffy* and *Toilet Central*. Funny and rude – and you can watch it over and over again.

Dispersion www.eiu.org/experiments/dispersion

A graduate computer science student, Eric Paulos, is trying to challenge the line between art and science and between performance and research. The majority of his efforts seem to be through this website, which claims to be 'Your easy one stop choice for personal lethal biological pathogens'. The gist is that it's installation art revolving around the design of vending machines for lethal human pathogens, or something.

Dumbentia   www.dumbentia.com

It's a sure sign that the boss has been on an evangelical-style motivation course when those dreadful posters start appearing on the wall behind their desk instructing people to bring them 'Solutions, not problems' and suggesting other ways of allowing them to avoid doing any work. The office sweatshop can even the score with a set of *de*motivational posters in beautiful eighties airbrush effect for each of the seven deadly sins.

Hell.com   www.hell.com

This is an artist web project with a presumably highly sought-after web address. The offers to buy the name should be flooding in.

The Incomplete   http://users.erols.com/
History of Art   browndk/art.htm

One man's mission to relieve people of the ignorance of the art world in a way they'll understand. His chosen method is to explain his own personal favourite parts by photographing re-enactments by Barbie dolls. Is that art in itself? Or dumbing down education? Or time to buy a book on the subject? Only a trip to this site will answer these questions.

Jones Town Re-enactment   www.jonestownreenactment.org

The debate over whether the nation's artists are a bunch of insane, lazy dole scroungers isn't going to be decided by this little activity. Ron Dickinson is trying to recruit people to perform in his re-enactment of a religious mass suicide that claimed the life of over 900 people in Guyana. The potentially weak plot with a predictable ending isn't going to ingratiate it to potential audiences, but there's sure to be plenty of Lottery money flowing his way.

Media Boy · www.mediaboy.net

This experience is guaranteed to embarrass any office worker having a sneaky peek at the web at work. Hundreds of windows pop up without any way of stopping them, flash a bit and then disappear all of a sudden. This could well be *the* most annoying site on the web.

Museum of Web Art · www.mowa.org

Unintentionally cheesy design to mimic a genuine art gallery and full of exhibitions. Very strange is the examination of animated web buttons. Beret and smock pretensions for the Internet generation.

The Museum of Bad Art · www.glyphs.com/moba

TMOBA is apparently both a community-based and private institution dedicated to the collection, preservation, exhibition and celebration of bad art in all its forms and in all its glory. Rather than just laughing at inept art, this site is a repository of work by talented artists who've stepped over the edge of sanity or were suffering from a temporary overexuberance with their brushes. Or it could be that the works are all the products of inebriation.

The Original Butt Sketch · www.buttsketch.com

A collective of artists who travel the world producing portraits of people's behinds. No explanation as to why they do this, but lots of examples of their 'work'. Find out when they'll be in your home town if you've always wanted a posterior portrait adorning your mantelpiece.

Roadside Art Online: Roadside Connections · www.interestingideas.com/roadside/artlink.htm

It's only fitting in the country of the car that there are so many interesting things to see out of the window that they should really be considered art. Check out bizarre billboards, strange buildings and monuments people have made in their gardens. Best of all is a huge page of links. Who said America was tacky?

Soulbath   www.soulbath.com

From the moment the URL is typed in the screen goes a bit weird, eventually getting to one simple command: 'Click here to start'. From that point on you are greeted with flashing, crashing screens that seem like they're never going to stop. Far out.

Stick Figure Death Theatre   www.sfdt.com

The place that animated stick figures meet their (quite literally) sticky ends. One gets shot, another run over and one's head explodes. Worth a visit for the review section, which includes some of the most self-indulgent literary ego massaging to be found this side of a newspaper letters page.

Superbad   www.superbad.com

We're talking *Shaft*, not a telling off from Grandma, here. The experience is a bit like a magical mystery tour through the mind of a sixties acid casualty. An utterly pointless and random experience with the upside that you're treated to some exquisitely cool visuals, but ultimately you feel that you've been nowhere.

Culture

Culture is like air: it's all around us and nobody can see it. The nineties seemed to be the point at which culture ran out of ideas and employed a consultant to rehash and mix all the old stuff and pack it up in a new glitsy package. The following is a random selection of what's out there:

80s Nostalgia   www.80snostalgia.com

Rolled-up jacket sleeves and designer lager live for ever here. If the me, me, me eighties were your bag and you can't quite get to grips with modern living, then this is the place to relax. You can even find out what was happening on this day in every day of the decade.

The Adventures of   www.cripworld.com/
Beverlee   beverlee/beverlee.htm
A fascinating web soap featuring an amputee Barbie doll constantly being stalked by her own Ken.

Alt.culture   www.altculture.com
A research project claiming to span the nineties youth culture and is moving nicely into the naughties with a daily email addition. Great explanations of grunge and gangsta, indie rock and indie film, cyberpunk and street fashion, extreme sports and political correctness, infomercials and ezines. Never be at a loss in fashionable company again.

Bad Fads   www.badfads.com
If the insidious postmodernism of the modern day has infiltrated all aspects of popular culture, it's reassuring to remember some of the more 'original' fashions of yesteryear for the complete abominations that they were. Ironing hair, poodle skirts and Bermuda shorts are all firmly off fashion's current agenda – but for how long?

The Book of   http://utopia.knoware.nl/users/
Clichés   sybev/cliche/cliche.htm
Whenever anything bad happens there's always someone on hand to mutter some dreadful cliché, as if it were going to make everything all right. Anyone with aspirations to be that person but finds themselves hampered by a short memory can print out a few of these pages and stand around waiting for disaster to happen.

Cockney Online   www.cockney.co.uk
Leave it out! Cor, blimey, guvnor! Cockles, pearly kings, insane bigoted cabbies – learn how to be a proper Londoner at the cockney HQ. Alternatively, just watch a couple of episodes of *EastEnders*.

CourtesyFlush.com   www.courtesyflush.com
Having problems with not knowing how to behave? Politically correct
or 'new lad'? Well this is where all today's etiquette questions are
answered – from using dessert forks to raising poodles.

Crappy Poetry   www.crappypoetry.com
Laugh at excruciating verse from broken-hearted tender types. It's
not very fair but it is very lame and funny.

Culture Jammers' Encyclopedia   www.syntac.net/hoax
The worthy hobby of culture jamming tries to devise perfect pranks
that approach a sublime art form. Those lacking in imagination but
with a mysterious itch waiting to be scratched can just pick a prank
to needle 'The Man'.

Ditherati   www.ditherati.com
A daily quote from a new media player. The new media industry has
recently overtaken the property industry as the prime producer of
corporate bullshit and a trip here every day will probably confirm
that they're getting worse.

Evil Overlord   http://minievil.eviloverlord.com/
list   lists/overlord.html
Imagine waking up one day to find that you were an evil overlord.
What do you do when the world is your oyster? Well, a good start is
to scan this list put together by this power-hungry bully victim.

15 Minutes of Shame   www2.ucsc.edu/~thebrain/shame
A site dedicated to nobodies who get fame through the power of
the TV camera – 'berated' into categories by the amount of fame
they managed to milk out of their individual predicaments. Check
out the rankings of those long-forgotten zeros, such as the security
guard who *didn't* bomb Olympic park, David Koresh and that top
(rich) nob-gobbler Divine Brown. For those on the cutting edge of
popular culture, keep abreast of up-and-coming nobodies with the
'Shamewatch' column.

Fuckwits
www.fuckwit.tm

Apparently, this is an expression invented by Australians. The characters responsible for this utterly pointless site have obviously been accused of being the very same thing on a number of occasions, and simply take this opportunity to list email addresses of people they deem worthy of the honour.

Gentlehints
www.gentlehints.com

Feeling a bit bashful about telling one of your mates that he hums like a rotting carcass? Well, Gentlehints will write them a nice little note to spare your blushes.

German UFO Watch
www.aircooledmind.org/aliens.html

A great conspiracy slant. UFOs are actually highly modified VW Beetles and Campers. A disgruntled American researcher in cahoots with the SS forms a secret, slave-labour, manufacturing plant in Antarctica. The evidence is there to see when famous UFO sighting pictures are subjected to image analysis.

I Hate Clowns
www.ihateclowns.com

Clowns have got a bad rap of late. They used to bring a smile to the face of kids the world over. After a couple of slasher movies kids are now steered well clear of them. The owner of this site absolutely can't stand them and wants the world to rise up against them. He even offers a free email service.

Manly Web
www.manlyweb.com

A hairy-arsed site for real men who drink beer and letch at babes. Wimps need not enter because the daily news about power tools, fast cars and steak eating just isn't going to interest them.

Nuke Pop
www.wsu.edu/~brians/nukepop

When the first nuclear bombs were dropped on Hiroshima and Nagasaki, popular culture was quick to respond. This is an examination of how living with the threat of global apocalypse during the Cold War years had a profound effect on the arts.

Ribbon Campaign   www.gargaro.com/ribbonstxt.html

It's not just jacket lapels that can wear good-cause ribbons. Websites do as well. Do a bit of good work for charity on your site by checking out this page and finding the ribbon of your favourite cause.

Save the Suburbanites   www.savethesuburbanites.com

Shameless white-collar begging from middle-class couple who frankly can't be bothered to work any more. They promise not to do anything but spend frivolously any donations that come their way. In reality they're waiting for Bill Gates to free them of their suburban chains and bestow a life of leisure on them. It's got to be worth a try.

A Sherlockian   http://waserv1.uwaterloo.ca/
Homepage   ~credmond/sh.html

If the strange, pipe-smoking, tweed-clad Baker Street dweller still rocks your world, then you'll probably agree that Chris Redmond's setup is the best Sherlock Holmes site out there. Links to all the others who mention their hero.

Tales From the Hellmouth   www.hellmouth.org

Whenever old folk wax lyrical about school days being the best of your life, greet them with a yawn. School in the States is now all about drive-bys, metal detectors, guns and massacres. One person decided enough is enough and decided to document the true horror of school days.

Un-American Activities   www.unamerican.com

While English-style culture imperialism is viewed as merely quaint by the outside world, the American equivalent is downright overbearing. The collective behind Un-American Activities don't have much time for the American *Zeitgeist*. They spread their message through lots of shouty ranting and some of the most eye-catching sloganeering on posters and merchandising ever produced.

Urban Legends Archive   www.urbanlegends.com

Urban legends are great because they've just about got enough plausibility to be true and everyone is just dying to believe them. These compendiums will arm the pub bore with stories for many a night's boozing.

Urban Legends Reference Pages   www.snopes.com

Brought to you by the San Fernando Valley Folklore Society, this site has a handy database search facility and features such as 'Critter County', 'Pregnancy' and 'Cokelore'. Relax here after finding out that nobody is sending sponges saturated with deadly 'Klingerman virus' in the post.

You Might Be a   http://vulcan.wolfcrews.com/
Yuppie Biker If . . .   misc/yuppie.htm

The weekend warriors of the ad world took to Harleys like ducks to water and soon the streets of big cities were awash with corpulent execs wobbling down the road on overdressed Hogs. If you drink cappuccino instead of beer or if your tattoos wash off, then you may have found soul mates here.

Goths

Remember those weedy, black-clad kids at school? Even though they never went away, people stopped noticing them. Well, they're back in force now, communicating through thousands of websites and chat rooms and their force is getting stronger.

Dress Trent   www.personal.psu.edu/users/m/j/
Reznor up   mjf195/music/trivial/paperdolls

Trent is the creative force behind the *über*-goth band Nine Inch Nails. A hero to many and one of the greatest exponents of whingeing the world has ever seen. Now there's no need to wait for a live show to sample his bizarre stage outfits, because you can dress him to your own tastes.

Gothic Babe of the Week   http://industrialgothic.com/gbotw
Sort of a Page 3 for the dark hordes. Check out the pasty-faced, big-haired girls who would like nothing more than to be mistaken for witches. Even better, tally up how many of them list poetry among their hobbies.

How to Design   http://meltingpot.fortunecity.com/
a Goth Website   oltorf/132/gothicy.htm
The first point of contact if you want to gingerly make moves out of your poster-clad bedrooms. There's an unnerving theme going on with goth websites and one trip to this instruction manual will explain why.

Jesus Was More   http://fox.nstn.ca/
Goth Than You   ~daveman/jesus
If Jesus's actions can be interpreted as his being a gun freak, vegetarian, republican, then there's no reason why he can't be considered to have been a proto-goth. After all, he was obsessed with death, harangued by trendy types, and big on crucifixes and piercings.

Tamagothi   www.gothic.net/~luvcraft/
     tamagothi/tamagothi.html
Equality for all in the late twentieth century meant that there was a cyber-pet for any culture. The nature-or-nurture debate can be put to rest permanently by Bela Lugosi fans with a penchant for pointy boots and crimped hair and a Tamagothi. A throbbing skull hatches on the chimes of midnight, at which point children of darkness can influence a childhood that would put Roseanne's to shame and could keep a generation of American therapists in loafers. With the right combination of narcotics, beatings, light depravation and isolation, the charge will develop into a top-grade, suicidal, angst-ridden goth who may even pen some dismal poetry.

See also 'Gothic gardening' in Chapter 5.

5//AT HOME

Considering that accessing the web is becoming almost as popular at home as it is in the office, it's no great surprise that everyday household objects are going to get the web treatment. There are plenty of people out there simply dying to help you make your living environment a little better or offering to sell you products that you never knew you needed.

Aircraft Homes   **www.maxpoweraero.com/ACHomes.htm**

If the missile silo isn't a wacky enough idea how about 'The Fastest House In The Housing Industry . . .'? Max Power Aerospace sells Boeing 727s as private residences. Just try finding somewhere to park it.

The Bathroom Habits   **www.cs.ualberta.ca/**
Study   **~davidson/bathroom**

As a subject unfitting for most polite conversations, this survey sets out to get to the bottom of the world's undercarriage cleaning habits. The site's comments book is essential reading for toilet-lovers everywhere.

Bizarre Stuff You Can   **http://freeweb.pdq.net/**
Make in Your Kitchen   **headstrong**

Whip up something really special in the kitchen. Whether you want fun making goo or to try your hand at homemade stink bombs, this guide is guaranteed to leave the place looking as if a bomb had hit it.

The Blenderphone   **www.cycoactive.com/blender**

Ultimate wedding present for fashion victims. A household blender with a phone built in so that margarita time is never disturbed by badly timed phone calls.

Electronic Bidet   www.sandman.com/intimst.html

Apparently the world's best toilet seat. A genuine product for the commode cognoscenti. No word of what happens if it malfunctions, though.

Goddess of Garbage   www.goddessofgarbage.com

Carol Tanzi is the self-proclaimed design-it-yourself diva and she's finding treasures in those rubbish bins. A must for style-obsessed student types.

Gothic Gardening   www.gothic.net/~malice

For nocturnal types intent on mending their ways. Handy tips on growing black roses and deadly nightshade to turn any garden into a spooky wilderness. (See also the 'Goths' section in Chapter 4.)

The Original World Famous Home   www.csn.net/~dcbenton/
Appliance Shooting Page   has.html

Daniel C Benton Jr is a master of destruction. Taking Elvis's hobby of TV shooting to its logical conclusion Mr Benton demonstrates how to blast the hell out of any television before moving on to other familiar household appliances.

Painted Potties   www.paintedpotties.com

If the rest of the house is perfect and the only thing that doesn't speak your personality is the toilet, then point wallets in this direction. Stickers for the porcelain throne that will hold fast for six months.

Piddlers Toilet Targets   http://silly-goose.com

Toilet-training aids to help toddlers make that difficult leap from potty to porcelain. Floating targets to pee on. Direct hits cause them to disintegrate, a bit like chasing a fag butt around a pub urinal.

Reverse Address   http://in-110.infospace.com/
Lookup   info/revaddr.htm

Due to hit the UK soon but presently only works for US and Canadian addresses. If you live in a city and you've wondered who your furtive neighbours are then this is how you can find out. Minutes of pleasure.

75 Years of Band Aid   **www.savetz.com/bandaid**

When the owner of this site bought his Northern Californian house from a friend's family he made a strange discovery. In the garage he found a collection of Band Aid boxes dating all the way back to the fifties. Like all good old timers, the previous owners had been loath to throw anything away and had kept knick-knacks in these old boxes. Find out what they kept.

Spork   **www.spork.org**

Designer cutlery or pointless kitchenware? A combination spoon and fork to help cut down on washing up and baffle guests.

Toilet   **http://kreskrafts.homestead.com/**
Podium   **toiletpodium.html**

A mini, church-style podium with built-in toilet-paper dispenser, hand-crafted in solid oak. Place your book or magazine on the top and settle in for a darn good read. The ideal wedding present for people you don't like – just imagine the combination of horror and confusion.

When Good Toilets   **http://home.att.net/**
Go Bad   **%7Etoyletbowlbbs/toilets.htm**

It's a horrible thought but they can bite back, and this collection of lavatorial stories, definitions and links is so compelling that you'll be hard pressed to leave.

World of Bad Taste,   **www.geocities.com/**
Bad Design and Kitsch House   **SoHo/Gallery/1553**

They publish design magazines so that your house doesn't end up like this. Not a single item inside World of Bad Taste, Bad Design and Kitsch House should ever make it to your domicile. All the items on display are the visual equivalent of sticking your fingers down your throat.

The World's Only Missile Silo   **www.missilebases.com/**
Luxury Home with Runway   **new**

What do you do with an $18 million missile silo after it's been decommissioned? If you're an enterprising estate agent you flog it off as a 'truly unique concept in modern living'. Not such a bad idea considering that there's no chance of getting burgled and it's even got its own runway.

Xtreme Blender   **www.xtremeblender.com**
The world's only food processor especially designed for bikers. Just like the real thing with a fearsomely powerful motor and on its own chrome podium with handlebars. No leather jacket required.

6//CELEBRITIES

The web is the perfect way for fans to show their appreciation of their idols, or disdain for their detractors. From gushing fan sites that consist of badly scanned-in magazine photos to full-on stalker-territory efforts, these sites have unwittingly become part of a star's promotional repertoire. It seems that someone's fame can now be measured by the number of adoring fan sites. On the other hand, far more amusing are the sites dedicated to attention-seeking media parasites which poke fun without remorse.

Actors With Skin Conditions   **www.ucsf.edu/~vcr**
Ha! So they're not that beautiful and godlike after all. Actors With Skin Conditions is a wince-inducing compendium of thesps' dermatological predicaments, bafflingly compiled by a genuine doctor.

André the Giant Has a Posse   **www.obeygiant.com**
A bizarre art experiment known as phenomenology aims to get the huge features of the now dead actor and wrestling star universally recognised through a sticker-and-poster campaign – and everyone's invited.

Areaology   **http://areaology.terrashare.com**
Early in 1997 Troll T Trull, the grandfather of modern areaology, asked himself this question: 'What if the entire physical universe and all the philosophical planes of existence are just a minuscule speck in one man's crotch?' He convinced himself that it was the truth and that the crotch belonged to David Bowie. Thus Ziggy Stardust's lunch box is omnipresent, or something.

Bert Is Evil   **http://fractalcow.com/bert/bert.htm**
We have reason to believe that Bert of *Sesame Street* fame is evil and you should keep your children away from him. Here in these pages are collected incriminating images and documents that prove

that Bert is not the lovable harmless geek he so successfully makes us think he is. Photo evidence includes Bert looking furtive at the front of the crowd just seconds before the Kennedy assassination, at the right hand of the *Führer* and leading Ernie astray in a lap-dancing club. Finally, as if more proof were needed, an intercepted email correspondence with Jeffrey Dahmer.

Bill Hicks   www.billhicks.com
The king of ranting, seething black comedy thankfully lives on through this website. The only man who can ever be forgiven for sporting a mullet haircut.

Celebrity Find a Grave   www.findagrave.com
Ever wondered where the heroes of yesterday currently reside? Look no further than this site. Apparently, they're now expanding our horizons and listing the graves of the nonfamous.

Charles Manson   www.charlesmanson.com
Not a true site for one of the best-known serial killers of the century. Social outcasts looking for a truly unique email address can sign up for a Manson one.

Charlie Bronson   www.charlie-bronson.com
The most dangerous man in Britain is a seventeen-stone, bodybuilding ex-wrestler who took his name from the actor. He has a habit of taking fellow prisoners and guards hostage and threatening to eat them. He's currently incarcerated and on an anger-management course. This is his world.

Compendium of   www.geocities.com/
Elvis Sightings   Hollywood/Set/1061
How can the King be dead. He obviously faked his own death when the pressures of fame got too much for him. OK, so he really did croak on the toilet but his army of fans won't let him go that easily and are always spotting rhinestone-clad men with sideburns in the most unlikely places (the men, that is, not the sideburns). If you find

that it's a little hard to believe that he's living in a small Mississippi town, upstairs at Graceland, in Vologda, Russia, or working as a sperm donor, then download the special Elvis Detector.

David Copperfield   **www.dcopperfield.com**
There's a dearth of electronic postcards to commemorate every special occasion, but what do you send someone you really hate? It's going to be hard for anyone to keep their breakfast down when greeted with a screen full of the King of Illusion himself. The real mystery is, of course, his ability to pull supermodels.

Divine Wind: Flatulence of   **http://web-star.com/**
the Rich and Famous   **divine/wind.html**
Admit it – anal eruptions are funny and they don't get any funnier than when they issue from the rear end of overpaid celebrities. For example, Oprah Winfrey during her liquid-diet phase, Roseanne packing a wallop, OJ Simpson blowing town and Michael Jackson's moonwalk serenade. For, as we all know, it is an ill wind that blows no good.

Driveways of the Rich and Famous   **www.driveways.com**
Celebrity stalking sites don't come much lamer than Driveways of the Rich and Famous, a homage to celebrity asphalt redeemed only by a profanity-laden transcript recalling an encounter with David Hasselhoff. Enough to turn milk sour . . .

Edward Woodward's   **www.conubic.com/eqew/**
Writing Room   **eq-ew/ewpstcrd.html**
Blue-rinse net heads may favour a card from that geriatric dreamboat and star of the highly unlikely series *The Equaliser*. Guaranteed to brighten the day of any octogenarian. Let's not forget he's best known as the actor who comes with free, built-in triple alliteration.

Elvis's Weight on the Other Planets at the Time of his Death
www.meyercom.com/public/what_the/fatelvis.htm

Fortunately, there's a handy clip-and-save chart of Elvis's weight on other planets. That's 648 pounds on Jupiter and a mere thirteen on Pluto. Proof that the whole issue of being overweight really is all relative.

Evel Knievel
www.evel1.com

The online home of the world's greatest ever daredevil – or at least one of the most spectacularly brave (or dumb) people ever. During a recent hospitalisation he even managed to post daily health updates. They don't make 'em like this any more.

The Exon awards
www.watchingyou.com/award.html

Join the overly sensitive Nebraskan ex-senator James Exon, one of America's more vociferous web opponents, and share a few of his thoughts on sites that have offended him recently.

Feed Celine Dion
http://egomania.nu/celine.html

It's oft remarked that the fatter her wallet becomes the more diminutive her dress size. Feed Celine Dion pleads with her fans to help her back to corpulent rude health. Those less than enamoured would probably suggest they keep feeding her wallet.

The Flying Elvi
www.flyingelvi.com

What weighs eighteen stones, is covered in rhinestones and Brylcreem and falls out of the sky? One of the Flying Elvi, of course! The team of sky-diving Elvis impersonators, who appeared in the film *Honeymoon In Vegas*, now have their own website. With facts, figures, pictures and, more importantly, how to book them for your next party. Garnished lovingly with an ultra-cheesy backing tune of 'Return To Sender' played on a Hammond organ.

Former Child Star Central http://members.tripod.com/ ~former_child_star

Child stars – one minute they've got everything, then they get a drug addiction or eating disorder, and then they get arrested, and then they've got nothing. Fortunately, they can then bask in obscurity. Not any more. This is a catalogue of the failed lives of these heroes of yesterday, available for all the world to see, and users are even encouraged to contribute public sightings.

George Foreman www.georgeforeman.com/

The boxer with the never-ending career has hit cyberspace. This site is full of the usual boxer preening; but, with retirement presumably looming at some point, he's branching out into his own products. Particularly amusing is the Lean Mean Fat Reducing Grilling Machine, available to buy through the site.

The Infamous Brad Pitt equalisation device www.watchingyou.com/ brad.html

Brad Pitt – the hunkiest man in Hollywood! For over a decade he's made millions of women swoon. A bunch of disgruntled boyfriends have decided to get even. By clicking the links the world can be reminded of Brad's looks before he'd even heard of a stylist.

Jay's Kids www.jayskids.com

Since his death in 1999, there's been a real-life hunt to locate the children of the legendary rhythm-and-blues singer Screamin' Jay Hawkins. By his own estimation he fathered 57 children, proving that the rock'n'roll lifestyle didn't start in the sixties.

Jolene's Trailer Park Heaven www.jolenestrailerpark.com

Jolene Sugarbaker is a self-proclaimed 'Fashion Consultant for All Mobile Home Owners in the World' and her lifestyle tips are essential viewing for wannabe white-trash aficionados everywhere. No aspect of this unenviable lifestyle is left uncovered. Start off by learning how to do your hair, yard and some basic cooking.

Julio Iglesias's Prom Planning Calculator for Boys
www.chickenhead.com/julio

One glance at this will have middle-aged spinsters the world over weeping into their Malibus and his lawyers browsing powerboat catalogues. This nifty little number claims to have all the information to set hormonal teenagers racing outdoors for a night of pubescent magic!

Lemmy speaks
www.imotorhead.com/ask.htm

Don't sit around wondering what type of drugs to take when listening to Motorhead. Ask Lemmy. For pure rock'n'roll advice, ask the warty rock trooper at the official site.

The Leonardo Di Caprio Unofficial Poetry Site
www.geocities.com/Paris/Parc/6560

Teenage angst may be unbearably unpleasant at the time – as acne is – but when it's a distant memory it's great for a few belly laughs. The Leonardo Di Caprio Unofficial Poetry Site is put together with so much sincerity it hurts. Raise a smile by emailing someone the heartfelt ode 'The Day I Fell In Love With Leo', and plenty of others.

The Lipstick Librarian
www.teleport.com/~petlin/liplib

For the lover of understated glamour and the man who knows that the quiet ones are always the worst. Rammed with hearty tips for the unassuming office vamp who knows that she's just got to break out of the oppressive corporate world in search of a bit of glamour.

Marry Tom Arnold
www.marrytom.com

After being turfed out on his ear by Roseanne, Tom Arnold is searching for a bride. All he's looking for is an adult single woman of child-bearing age, good with children, willing to relocate, has goals, and is self-confident enough to wear a bathing suit on vacation. Send in any suggestions, and lucky winners may win a date with Tom himself.

Meet Art Fry   www.3m.com/Post-it/artslab/meet_art_fry.html

Briefly adorning offices throughout the world before being blown into the unknown by cranky air-conditioning units, the humble sticky note is familiar throughout the world. Art Fry is the genius who thought of combining glue that wasn't sticky and small pieces of yellow paper. This is his world.

Michael Moore   www.michaelmoore.com

Former car worker, broadcaster and political agitator, Michael Moore is carrying on his anticorporate activities from his cyber home.

Mr T vs.   www.angelfire.com/ca3/
Britney Spears   tfiles/britney.html

Comic-book action as the Louisiana teen temptress dares to take on the mythical A Team superhero.

Pimptopia   www.pimptopia.com

Ever noticed how actors look just like pimps? Fantastic unintentional pimp moments from Hollywood's finest.

Pottyticians   http://members.spree.com/
jdever/pottyticians.htm

While most people like to see politicians disgraced and humiliated, most would draw the line at seeing them on the toilet. Do the business with Bill Clinton and other world leaders.

Quotes From   www.dtcc.edu/~rod/
Supermodels   supermodel.html

The widely perceived notion that supermodels are superfluous, vacuous bits of human fluff isn't exactly challenged by Quotes from Supermodels. Then again, laughing at people who are richer and better looking than mere mortals isn't exactly going to rob them of any unneeded beauty sleep.

The Real Monica Inc   www.therealmonicainc.com

Now all the brouhaha about that little bit of work experience that she did in the White House has died down, Monica Lewinsky has settled down to a nice sensible career. Nobody is going to guess what she's up to now.

The Scullywear   http://members.aol.com/
Auxiliary Brigade   scullywear

Gillian Anderson attracts her fair share of sci-fi stalkers and this effort is particularly worrying. The SAB have dedicated themselves to chronicling their icon on her numerous public appearances and screen outings.

Speakin'   http://dspace.dial.pipex.com/log/
Deacon   joeydeacon/joeytalk.htm

A homage to Joey Deacon, *Blue Peter*'s part-time presenter in the seventies. With authentic audio, an altogether monstrously cruel endeavour.

Teri Hatcher   www.geocities.com/Hollywood/
In Trouble   Boulevard/3656

Dungeons and Dragons has a lot to answer for, particularly this site. The damsel-in-distress scenario has been given a modern lick of paint. This is a collection of stills of Teri Hatcher featuring her in numerous potential rescue situations. All she needs is to be rescued by a geek armed with a raspberry-coloured iMac.

The Nun Who Appeared in a Bun   www.bongojava.com

Ryan Finney, an employee of a Nashville coffee house, was tucking into his mid-morning snack when he noticed an alarming similarity between it and the Holy Mother of Calcutta. At this point the American hype machine lurched into action and the phenomenon of the NunBun was born, culminating in the making of a film, *A Music City Miracle: The Story of The NunBun*.

Timothy Leary; Chaos Without And Within   www.leary.com

He may be gone, his ashes blasted into outer space, years after his mind arrived there, but his spirit and philosophies live on. Meet up with the psychedelic professor in his new home in cyberspace and find out why he wasn't your run-of-the-mill sixties hippie but a cornerstone of the counterculture revolution.

Uri Geller   www.uri-geller.com
The world's most famous spoon bender has never been known for his modesty. This official site has you thinking he's the Second Coming with plenty of fascinating stories and commendations from scientists and other notables.

What If They   www.nbc.com/NBCconan/
Mated?   index.asp?section=mated
Try to imagine what the offspring of some of today's celebrity couples would look like if, heaven forbid, they had kids. Gruesome.

Who Would You Kill?   www.whowouldyoukill.com
Go one better than screaming at the TV screen when overpaid, smug celebrities disrupt your evening's viewing pleasure. This is where irritating TV celebrities get their comeuppance. Users get to vote on who is the most disliked member of the cast on the US's top shows and if your show's not there then suggest one.

William Shatner   www.hecklers.com/simshatner/
Acting Simulator   simshatner.php3
Think you're up to getting your shirt ripped in fights and copping off with foxy aliens? Find out by taking control of the bridge and strutting your best Captain Kirk stuff.

World Famous Society for Future   www.sfhbs.com/
Husbands of Britney Spears   home
The jailbait star Britney Spears seems to do strange things to many males' hormones. This particular fan site is like a gathering point for potential stalkers and sex pests who are going to torment her until the next teen sensation breaks cover. So join the acne-and-Kleenex brigade here.

7//COLLECTIONS

Collecting is a fine hobby. It's not time-sensitive, so you don't have to try too hard or be too productive. It doesn't require physical prowess or generally any form of human contact. From those devoted to collections of great works of art to those who love trainspotting, collecting fans are everywhere and almost always male. They went about their collecting almost unnoticed, apart from the occasional sighting or documentary, until the web became their own glass-fronted cabinet to show off all their treasures. It's a bit disturbing to find out that there are a lot of these people about – a lot more than we ever knew existed.

Air Sickness Bag Virtual Museum   www.airsicknessbags.com
Apparently, it's possible to tell a lot about an airline's image from their air sickness bags. Some bags are no more than a baggie with a twist tie, while others could win international design competitions. Are they art? This guy thinks so. Amazingly, he's never been out of the USA.

The Amazing Rubber   www.easttexas.com/
Band Ball   pdlg/theball.htm
One man's obsession with keeping rubber bands together. This is a hobby that should exist only within an office environment. There's even an address to send donations.

Burlingame Museum of   www.spectrumnet.com/
Pez Memorabilia   pez/pezexhibit.html
Monstrous collection of Pez dispensers from a man who's probably fifty stone and lost his teeth. If this is Burlingame's No. 1 tourist attraction – just drive on through.

The Burns Street museum   www.badburns.bizland.com
Sideburns have been sneaking back quietly since they were banished from acceptable fashion in the eighties. With explanations

and historical descriptions of the 'ultimate symbol of masculinity' to photo galleries of famous 'burns victims' (there've been a few), this is an unashamed tribute to the mighty sideburn.

The Complete List of Famous Belgians
http://ourworld.compuserve.com/homepages/Tielemans/hp4marc.htm

What seems like an ambitious task is hampered by the relative lack of celebrities. This list could come up with only 242 of them.

Corkscrew
www.corkscrew.com

A not-so-fascinating site built by and dedicated to a San Francisco Bay area couple's twenty-year passion for collecting corkscrews. Drinking wine is a far better hobby.

Erik's Chopstick Gallery
www.ichizen.com/chopsticks

Erik Wegweiser decided that he wanted to collect something that was truly different. He decided that Pokémon cards, Beanie Babies or hamburger freebies weren't good enough, so he decided to collect chopsticks. Two sticks to eat food with and so many different types. Erik's profession is – surprise, surprise – computer consultancy.

Fast Food Toy Museum
http://members.dencity.com/happymeal

Junk-food junkie proudly displays his free gifts. Truly limited culinary horizons, but they have their own limited benefits.

Flash Mountain
www.thatguy.com/splash

There can't be many people who haven't flicked a V sign when they've seen themselves on a video monitor. Stateside, where everything has to be better, there seems to be a new craze sweeping Uncle Walt's World. Naughty people have been flashing their bodies as the camera fires at the scariest point of the Splash Mountain ride. Staff are supposed to censor these naughty pictures but quite a few seem to have got out and found their way on to the web. Worth a visit for the match-the-body-parts game.

Goatee Gallery　　　　www.bluecalabash.com.au/goatee/
After years of male facial hair being relegated to the same fashion
bin as leg warmers, Kurt Cobain and his grunge foot soldiers took
the humble goatee beard back from wizards and real-ale fans and
put it across even the glossiest fashion spreads. Now they're
relegated to extreme sports fans and famous serial killers. This is the
result of one man's obsession.

The Incredible World　　　　www.feargod.net/
of Navel Fluff　　　　fluff.html
Gruesomely featuring the world's biggest and longest-term
collection of one person's navel fluff, which took over sixteen years
to amass. Ear wax beckons . . .

It Crawled From　　　　www.phoenixnewtimes.com/
the Bins　　　　extra/gilstrap/crawl.html
One man's crusade to compile the world's worst record collection
seems to have been an overwhelming success. This is absolutely
horrifying. Jarvis Cocker himself would blush at its cheesiness. Not
for the faint of heart.

John's Beer-Drinking　　　　www.ucl.ac.uk/~ccaajpa/
Records　　　　beer-records.html
Sites like this can exist only on a college server. A complete list of all
the beers that the very proud owner has drunk since starting the
site. A truly momentous waste of taxpayers' money.

Keeping Ken　　　　www.manbehindthedoll.com
Ken, that perpetual appendage of Barbie, and his fashions through
the ages. Creepily maintained by Jef, a middle-aged man. Small
girls should accept no sweets from this man.

Lee's Superfine Banana
Label Collection　　　　www.overmann.org
One man's testament to his fibre intake. Saving the labels from
bananas may not be the ultimate action hobby but at least it's

healthy. Presumably, this is a superfine collection because the opposition isn't that strong.

Mate In a State   **www.mateinastate.com**
What better way of showing affection than to humiliate your friends in front of the whole world. Rather than look after drunk and incapable friends, take pictures of them and submit them to this site. Or even their favourite shots where they think they look cool. Needs an office-party section.

The Most Embarrassing   **www.buyafunnybook.com/**
Moment of my Life   **moments**
A collection of embarrassing stories with the option of submitting your own.

Museum of Dirt   **www.planet.com/dirtweb/dirt.html**
Collecting dirt isn't most people's idea of a great day out, but, as with most hobbies, it's hard to explain the attraction to the outside world. This site looks more like an excuse to do a bit of celebrity stalking and bring back a memento that won't involve the perpetrator winding up in court. Handfuls proudly on display include Sonny Bono's front yard, OJ's Rockingham Estate, Mick Jagger and Jerry Hall's flower bed and Gianni Versace's front steps.

My Homepage   **http://welcome.to/mytrailerparkpage**
Someone has found some pictures of the ugliest people on the planet and crafted this hilarious spoof series of web pages. It's a parody of every pointless personal webpage out there starting with the host introducing himself and then going on to introduce the rest of his gargoyle-like family in the most retarded trailer-trash dialect possible.

My Slide   **www.physics.ohio-state.edu/**
Rules   **~dvandom/slidegallery.html**
The reason that calculators were invented was to prevent people having to use these jumped-up little rulers. Slide rules are one of the

least user-friendly calculating devices ever conceived. Sure, they're clever, but so what? One man thinks that spending a pound on a cheap calculator in his local petrol station is not a patch on the venerable slide rule. This is his collection.

Old's-cool   **www.swint.demon.co.uk**

Remember when just walking past a naked flame was enough to turn you into a human fireball, in those good old days before clothes manufacturers had to obey any laws? Well, Nick Norton does and he wants to show off his collection of the uniform of British white trash – his 1970s and 1980s tracksuits.

Pylon of the Month   **www.pylonofthemonth.co.uk**

Cancer-causing blots on the landscape or beautiful monuments to man's conquest of nature and his advancing technology. Most people's dealings with electricity pylons have been limited to mild annoyance or the odd tut-tut, but one man wages a campaign of positive PR for the humble pylon, claiming that there's a 'fascinating and rewarding hobby of electricity pylon number collecting'. To avoid downpours and marauding cows, check out his efforts here.

Rectal Foreign   **www.well.com/user/**
Bodies   **cynsa/newbutt.html**

Proving that people putting strange objects up themselves isn't entirely the stuff of urban legend is the mission of this collection of X-rays and reports about people who've turned up in A & E because they've 'accidentally fallen' on something.

Sneaker Nation   **http://sneaker-nation.com**

The world of trainers. History and the best care tips. Popular culture has been fascinated by athletic footwear since kids started getting killed over them. This site offers a potted history and a selection of trainer-care tips.

Tacky postcard archive   **www.tackymail.com**
Electronic postcards with a difference. These all started life as badly designed real-world cards and have been lovingly scanned to preserve them for posterity. In their original incarnations they truly were a waste of ink.

Trolley Spots   **www.angelcities.com/members/trolleyspots**
Milton Keynes has been the brunt of the nation's jokes since it was invented in a test tube back in the seventies. All those trimmed lawns and unnecessary roundabouts now take a back seat to its 'trolley culture'. This new town is apparently a Bermuda triangle for every drunk student's favourite form of transport. They seem to be discarded with increasing frequency and one dedicated fan has catalogued all sightings and even named some of them. Look out for 'Crash Gordon', and 'Runway Steve'.

The Ultimate Bad Candy   **www.bad-candy.com**
BLAH (Boisterous Legion Against Healthy treats) are on a mission to seek out the most unpleasant sweets on the planet. Not for them the safety of food manufactured to government hygiene standards; only the most foul tooth rotters are good enough.

8//DAFT HUMOUR

There are jokes and throwaway lines that are side-splittingly funny that vanish from people's memories almost as fast as they appeared. Or that's what used to happen. Nowadays, these little quips based on a single idea form the basis of whole daft websites.

Aluminum foil deflector beanie   http://zapatopi.net/afdb.html
What all the best-dressed paranoiacs will be wearing this season. Stop the FBI listening to your thoughts with a foil hat. With step-by-step instructions. Never saw them making one of these on *Blue Peter*.

Cool Lego Site of the Week   www.lugnet.com/cool
Overgrown children seek praise from others of a similar disposition. Marvel at the Lego creations dreamed up by forty-year-olds who can't put a train set together.

Crank Dot Net   www.crank.net
A collection of sites devoted to the more gifted and eccentric members of the population. Claiming to be devoted to cranks, crankism, crankishness, and crankosity. Never be ignorant about urine therapy or time travel again.

Cruel Site of the Day   www.cruel.com
They really mean it – no beating about the bush. Eye-popping stuff every day.

Evil Cones   http://thunder.prohosting.com/~evil/
They're springing up everywhere. With every passing year there are more and more of them. Well, there's a reason for that: they're about to take over, and here's the proof.

EvilBastards.com   www.evilbastards.com
Free email with attitude. Annoy, amuse and upset your mail recipients by showing them you have no respect for civility.

Feral Cheryl   www.feralcheryl.com.au
A natural-looking doll toy from Australia that's a 'realistic portrayal of the feminine body'. She wears her alternative lifestyle with pride: she goes barefoot, has tattoos, dreadlocks and simple clothes, and carries a hand-made rainbow bag.

Joe's Amazing   www.execpc.com/
Problem Solvers   ~lungfish/probsolv
Sterling advice for people whose lives have reached a crossroads and they don't know which way to turn. Step-by-step problem solving in Original flavour as well as deluxe Relationship and Federal Government Problem Solver! After a barrage of 'Will you get away with it?' and being called an idiot, it's just possible that your original problem might not seem quite so bad, and a short course of therapy is the only way to sort out your head.

The Laser   http://omnibus.uni-freiburg.de/
Sword   ~jepsen/thz/lassword.htm
Get rid of post-birthday trauma after being presented with an 'authentic' light sabre. Even five-year-olds in the seventies weren't fooled by a torch with integral clear-plastic guttering. It's taken more than twenty years but German scientists claim to have developed the Laser Sword, and will probably make their fortunes at sci-fi conventions.

Lowbrow   www.lowbrow.com
Submit your lowbrow moment or, if you can't co-ordinate the keyboard, read others'.

Man-Eating Cabbage   http://miso.wwa.com/
Patch Dolls   ~jvitous/cp.htm
Vicious, man-made and on the rampage. Not 'Raptors on the attack but Man-Eating Cabbage Patch Dolls. You just never know what happens when the lights go out.

Nude Man www.maui.net/~liam/nudecarrot/
Carrot nudemancarrot.html
A carrot that looks like a nude man. Who'd have thought it? Now
he's got his own website.

Oo www.alcyone.com/oo
Things that make you go 'oo'. One syllable, thousands of uses. A
collection of stories, statements and words that make you go 'oo'.

People Who've Lost http://members.tripod.com/
Their Marbles ~abnorml/A.HTM
Insanity is an acceptable excuse, it seems, and heart can be taken by
joining other people who've lost their marbles, a self-help group for
the 'You Don't Have To Be Crazy . . .' type of office prankster.

Play With Lulu Doll www.futile.com/lulu
Lulu's not a Scottish singer with a long shelf life but a sinister-
looking green-faced doll. Moving the cursor around will make her
eyes roll in their sockets and various body parts move or swing.
Utterly pointless – but creepy.

Pooh Goes www.geocities.com/
Apeshit Colosseum/Base/9807/
He always was too nice. Find out what happens when he finally
cracks.

Raving Toy Maniac www.toymania.com
The magazine for your inner child. A wealth of childhood memories.

Slappingpappy www.slappingpappy.com
Vent that spleen on hapless celebrities with hundreds of slap-'em-
up games.

The Stupid Page www.sebourn.com/stupid.html
A compendium of pointless stories, product warnings, road signs,
bureaucratic cock-ups and strange things found in Tupperware to
make the modern idiot take heart that they're not inhabiting the
bottom of the food chain.

Superkaylo   **www.superkaylo.com**
Humour site, featuring lots of teenage lust with Horny Michelle.
Laugh at the cyber-twats. Best of all is Unnovations, fictional things
with no potential.

Transmissions from Quantum Time   **www.speakeasy.org/~z2013**
'We can contact you. We are your future mind.' Click a couple of
links into this one and you could end up at an 'official' Charles
Manson website. In the interests of a positive mental outlook, avoid
this like Chuck avoids sanity.

Wanker.org   **www.wanker.org**
A gang of angry gentlemen who spend their time ranting and
calling people rude names. Particularly harrowing is to be the
subject of Wanker of the Month.

9//EDUCATION

One of the foremost uses of the web was as an educational tool. With the number of sites dedicated to educating people of all ages, the web is the best way to go for self-improvement. It's like the ultimate textbook: you don't have to buy it and it's never going to go out of date. Quite how useful it is, however, is a matter of opinion, as these offerings will testify:

Beginners' Guide at   **www.head-space.com/**
the Circle Makers   **circlemakers**
Think of all the crackpot scientists trying to make sense of concentric circles in Kent wheat fields, how stupid they look now. Had they bothered to notice the Land Rover tracks or visited the Beginners' Guide at the Circle Makers site they would be a little more reticent about making fools of themselves in front of a camera.

Discover the   **www.yourcounsellor.bizland.com/**
Meaning of Life   **doorways/meaningot.html**
This site doesn't deliver quite what's expected. It offers to help unravel the mysteries of existence but it's just run by a load of psychologists on the make – a bit like Scientology really. Add to your troubles by being indebted to a load of opportunistic counsellors for the next few years.

Dissect   **http://curry.edschool.virginia.edu/**
a Frog   **go/frog/menu.html**
For the squeamish wimps of the class who can't stand the thought of hacking a poor frog to bits in science class, there's now an alternative. Virtual frog dissection over the web avoids all the smells and nastiness.

Learn How To Hunger Strike www.hungerstrike.com/askdoc.html

Essential guide for wannabe activists. Fortunately there's no mention of dirty protesting.

Learn to Play Air Guitar http://mirrorimage.com/air

Heavy-metal fans have long known that you can still be a rock god without all that tedious guitar practice. Mastering of the air guitar is not something that comes naturally but can be learned through these enlightening pages.

Manufacture an Alibi www.alibi.co.uk

Everybody gets themselves into a situation at some point from which they can extricate themselves only with a little white lie. The thing is, it has to be good and plausible, and that's why this is the site for one of those little crises.

Morbid Fact du Jour www.shocking.com/~despair/morbid.htm

One grisly fact per day for the gruesomely inclined sick little monkeys out there. The facts span several centuries and catalogue some blood-curdling events, including genocide, death rituals, random accidents, and unusual punishments.

Online Guide to Accident Preparedness www.accidentprep.com

Definitely one from the glass-half-empty brigade. There are a load of road accidents every day and this site is out to help you get ready for the inevitable. Download the simple checklist, print it out and keep it in the car for the next time you're feeling a little drowsy.

Risca Comprehensive School http://atschool.eduweb.co.uk/risca

Desperate attempt by a Welsh school to drum up numbers. This school lists some of its unique facts in an attempt to lure new pupils. Apparently there are 31 brown doors on the top floor and the teacher who lives nearest to the school is Mr Portsmouth.

S.T.U.P.I.D.   http://athena.athenet.net/~jlindsay/
PCPhysics.shtml

Forget night school: cutting-edge academia can be sampled with an intensive training in Politically Correct Physics. By enrolling at S.T.U.P.I.D. (Scientific and Technical University for Politically Intelligent Development), students can shoot down in flames the once sacrosanct ideologies that elbow-patched beardies have been peddling for generations. After a few lectures in White Male Oppression in Nuclear Physics, Quantum Mechanics: Contributions of Indigenous Peoples, Contributions of the Vertically Challenged in Physics, all rounded off with a smattering of Feminist Cosmology, antisocial individuals will lose the will to offend anyone.

Tomb of the Chihuahua Pharaohs   http://members.aol.com/
crakkrjack

As an exercise in making education more palatable, can diminutive dogs shed enlightenment on the secrets of Ancient Egypt? They seem to think so.

What To Bring With You When   www.loompanics.com/
You Go To Federal Prison Camp   federalprisoncamp.htm

With the majority of America's population currently residing at taxpayers' expense, this could be the best advice ever offered to stateside visitors. Jaywalkers beware – the three-strike rule leads to a mandatory life sentence, so it's a wonder that most students ever get through their freshers' week.

10//ENTERTAINMENT

With production costs being so cheap, websites have become a prime source of entertainment for the world. Fan sites for TV shows are plentiful, and there seems to be a never-ending source of animations that will never ever make it on to the nation's TV screens.

Television, the drug of the nation

With the web vying for screen eyeballs, there is inevitably going to be some crossover. There are thousands of tribute sites and a seemingly insatiable appetite for the nostalgia for the shows of the seventies.

Carry Online   **www.carryonline.com**
Oooh, Matron! Sid, Hattie, Babs and all the gang are immortalised at the online smut nirvana. Rammed full of more pictures, interviews and biographies than fans will find anywhere else. Sadly, the obituaries section seems to get longer by the day.

Chris Morris' Guff   **www.rethink.demon.co.uk/laugh.html**
It's about time that the most evil man in the media today got a decent web presence, and this is just that. Reliving former glories, which have subsequently barred him from just about every broadcaster in the land, this site has to be an essential stop-off for all his fans.

Dr Moose   **http://moose.spesh.com/teletubbies**
Had the BBC's costume designers confined their use of sponges to washing dishes and bathtime, the nation might have been spared TV's latest sensation. Unfortunately, they didn't, and our screens are graced with a show that resembles a care-in-the-community fancy-dress day out. Those absent for the departure of the

Teletubbies' boat may need to consult Dr Moose, who can explain how the mutant hell spawn of Mr Blobby came into existence.

Frank Butcher's Philosophical Car Lot
http://geocities.com/SunsetStrip/Stadium/1123/page1.html

Ow, Pat! *EastEnders'* tearful car dealer struts his funky stuff in his virtual car lot. Featuring sound clips of his favourite catchphrases, a variety of gruesome photos and, best of all, his alter ego Mike Reid's contribution to popular music in the 'Maim That Tune' section.

Freespeech Internet television
www.freespeech.org

The truth is out there and it doesn't involve overpaid actors chasing aliens. A genuine TV channel promoting global free speech.

Gunge in the UK
www.appz.demon.co.uk/gunge/gunge.htm

That British TV comedy mainstay so cruelly swept aside by trendy, lefty, so-called alternative comedians is preserved for posterity. The glory days of Flan Flying live on here.

The Jerrry Sticker Show
www.megsinet.net/~rlsweb/stick/jerry.htm

Watch the results of a bizarre collision between the Stick Figure Death Theatre and the undisputed king of tabloid TV on *The Jerrry Sticker Show*.

Mediawhores
www.mediawhores.co.uk

Containing disturbing images of TV celebrities and film stars. Well, a spoof night's viewing with some cunningly doctored images featuring celebrity head grafting.

Sausagenet
www.sausagenet.co.uk

Another step down memory lane for children of the seventies whose childhood entertainment consisted of being plonked in front of a TV set. This is the place to catch the theme tune to *Rent a Ghost* or *Jamie and the Magic Torch* and then follow the links to the fan sites.

TV Cream   www.tv.cream.org

Where cheesy British TV shows retire. Nostalgic tears will flow as treasures from *Tucker's Luck* to *Cheggers Plays Pop* are fondly remembered. Not content with TV shows, they're now branching out into adverts, films, magazines, radio, soft drinks and decrepit foodstuffs.

TV Go Home   www.tvgohome.com

Absolutely guaranteed not to make it to the small screen are the inclusions on TV Go Home. The biweekly updates simply consist of a parody of Britain's best-loved TV listings magazine. While the look may be familiar, the programmes will make your eyes pop.

TV Ultra   www.tvultra.com

If you'd like just to cut back on TV rather than go cold turkey, this is like a tube diet. Just one show daily for your fix, freeing up loads of time for inane web browsing.

Wild Feed TV   www.wildfeedtv.com/wftv/links.html

Eavesdropping on satellite feeds reveals some hilarious 'off-camera' moments. Watch a supermodel in action as Christy Turlington hones her acting skills in a challenging shoot for her new line in underwear.

Web 'toons

The popularity of the web can also be its downfall, as anyone who's tried to watch any video streaming has found to their cost. Animations on the web are another matter. Animators don't have to tout their services around the world any more: they can distribute and showcase through websites. There are literally thousands of cartoons out there with quality spanning the whole spectrum.

Airworld.net   www.airworld.net

Interactive artists have created the 'Jargon Machine', which
tirelessly patrols the web stealing ad copy, video and images from
real sites and then packages them into a nonsensical stream with all
company names being replaced with Airworld.

Heaven   www.icebox.com

Spoof of *Cheers*, where Mother Teresa, Einstein, Edgar Allan Poe,
Princess Di and a guy named Jake who didn't wear his seatbelt
spend eternity where the bar scene is really dead: JFK's Bar and Grill
in Heaven. Heaven's not what you thought, but at least you know
everybody's name.

Jonni Nitro   www.eruptor.com

Rather than create animations, this is actually filmed in real life and
then reduced to black and white. Follow the adventures of Jonni in
an online comic strip.

Like, News   www.shockwave.com

The news presented in a truly unique way by fourteen-year-old
Skeeter. Once it's been sampled, it'll be hard to go back to the dear
old BBC.

Open Mic   www.theromp.com

The animated alter egos of two real-life comedians who take part in
a weekly stand-off. The audience vote on who's the funnier, and
the eventual winner gets five thousand dollars. Stand up without
any chance of being picked out of the audience for humiliation.

Robot House   www.toonshack.com

A comedy sitcom about a bunch of robots who live in a suburban
ranch house. Lots of silly robot voices and hip references to popular
culture.

Spümcø Cartoons!   www.spumco.com

What's more fun than beer or sex education? This is! Home of one
of America's most subversive doodlers, John Kricfalusi. Who's he?

The man who persuaded Nickelodeon to buy his *Ren & Stimpy* cartoon. After a handful of episodes, they realised that a cartoon featuring a quest for a talking fart may be a bit much for Uncle Sam's next generation of Wall Street hotshots. He was out on his ear before Stimpy got a chance to reacquaint himself with his friends the nose goblins. Mr K won't be stung by multinational media companies again and is planning to distribute his work at low cost through this website. Catch a first glimpse of Jimmy the Idiot Boy, George Liquor (including a personal message), Jimmy's Pussy, Cigarettes the Cat, Nutty the Friendly Dump and Jimmy's underage girlfriend, Sody Pop. Don't let your parents find out about this one, kids.

The God and the Devil Show   www.entertaindom.com

Hugely corporate Time Warner entertainment portal, which is entirely redeemed by the inclusion of the wickedly funny *The God and Devil Show*. Each week the God and the Devil host a chat show with a celebrity. Particularly good is the Ron Jeremy episode.

Built for the web

It's not just 'toons that are being made specially for the web. There's a whole load of live-action shorts being made for the PC. TV scheduling is going to become a thing of the past as soon as people discover some of these entertaining efforts.

Atom Films   www.atomfilms.com

Loads of short films including Ben Affleck's *I killed my lesbian wife, hung her on a meat hook and now I have a three picture deal at Disney*. Unlikely to be previewing at your local multiplex.

The Couch   www.thecouch.com

An online serial that takes place in a Manhattan psychiatrist's office. Visitors are invited to eavesdrop on the neuroses and whining of a bunch of over-therapised New Yorkers. 'Squirt Down My Leg',

'Latte and Acid', and 'Good Drugs, Bad Sex' have been recent topics.

Culture Jam   www.culturejam.com
Check out the mockumentary, *Legally Dead*, about a serial killer who offs lawyers; and *Subway Map* explores what New York city graffiti would sound like.

Doll Soup   www.dollsoup.co.uk
A bad-taste soap opera with a cast of self-aware dolls. Follow the trials of postmodern Switch, brainless Leela and moralising Pam as they try to make it big in the city. Mental illness, cat-fights, evil cloned twins etc. etc.

The Junkies   www.thejunkies.com
The Junkies is a DIY comedy sitcom. There was no commissioning editor, no broadcaster and no top comedy company involved, just a team of people who worked for no money and very little food. Guess what the subject matter is about?

Kill Frog   www.killfrog.com
Daft animations including 'Star Word', 'The Paragraph Menace', 'Spin the Kitty', 'Lame Cyber Robots' and 'The Everloading Story'.

Panty Cat   www.kibo.com/exegesis/panty_cat.shtml
The characters of 'Quake' and 'Final Fantasy' aren't the most addictive creations of the video-game world, 'Panty Cat' is. With his 'real-time underwear strategy' he can be dressed in a stunning array of panties of your choice.

Polly and Esther   http://quality-schnallity.com/pollyesther.htm
A couple of tiresome spinsters, you know the ones that 'your parents force you to visit during spring break'. Well the reason for their strange antics is not that they're a bit eccentric but that they're brain-eating zombies.

Pseudo.com **www.pseudo.com**
Technophiles bored of waiting for the eagerly anticipated advent of interactive TV will be pleasantly surprised at what the web can offer. Pseudo.com is an interactive TV channel for the humble PC with a dozen daily shows boasting a slickness that most cable channels only strive for.

Shortbuzz **www.shortbuzz.com**
A collection of movie shorts with the kung-fu pizza-delivery boy flick *Better Never Than Late*. After watching this, you'll never forget to tip your local moped-riding road warrior again.

Tammy **www.tammyworld.com**
Trailer trash queen appears in her own online soap. Will she ever have her drunken way with the Michael Bolton loving sex god in trailer 31? Follow her white-trash adventures here for a drama that makes *EastEnders* look like the Waltons.

11//EZINES

Web pioneers claim that it's the greatest advance in human communication since the printing press. With practically no overheads, the budding media owner doesn't have to work for a corporation to be heard and has a platform with a cheap global reach. There are thousands of online magazines, or ezines, out there. Some are inspired, some tragic, but it does prove that ordinary people can be really quite funny.

Bitter Slut   **www.bitterslut.com**
A magazine for females who have been truly scorned. Revenge, rehabilitation and general letting off of steam.

Bizcotti   **http://bizcotti.com**
The best buzz in town from this entertainment ezine, some of the best Hollywood gossip around.

Bomb Dog   **www.dogbomb.co.uk**
Fifty per cent canine, fifty per cent explosive, one hundred per cent bizarre and totally ripped off from *The Day Today* TV show. Online humour zine.

Bringdown   **www.bringdown.com**
Claiming that it's published by 'a collective of San Francisco-based artists united to fight the hypocrisy of misinformation stemming from the continual conglomeration of media sources in our post-modern cultural environment'. Then admitting that it's actually cobbled together by 'just one lonely, cranky, grotesque individual who finds his biggest daily challenge is getting out of bed in the morning'. A fine effort.

The Brunching Shuttlecocks   **www.brunching.com**
Satirical ezine where entropy and irony live together in perfect harmony. The complete and utter idiot's guide to cooking a TV dinner and the Alanis Morisette lyric generator.

Bubblegun   **www.bubblegun.com**
'Where popular culture goes to die'. Including the web's best top tens, such as things to do in a posh restaurant. One visit will turn your life into a constant series of lists like a character in Nick Hornby's *High Fidelity*.

The Chap Magazine   **www.artfink.demon.co.uk/chap**
Rejoice in the death of new-lad culture and hail the rise of the old lad. A compendium of lifestyle tips harking back to finer times when manners really did maketh man. It's a celebration of all things elegant from a time when wearing a moustache was a fitting career for a man of leisure and smoking a pipe was an activity reserved for tobacco consumption and not the preserve of ruffians in alleyways. Highlights include the interactive 'Semiotics of Hair', 'Random Acts of Common Courtesy' and the adventures of Cecil de Cashmere.

Chicken Is Good Food   **www.chickenisgoodfood.com**
Not poking fun at vegetarians but a humour zine that includes crazy art, downloads, comics, links and general splurge-of-consciousness stuff.

CRAP   **www.crapcrapcrap.com**
Certified Renegade American Product, or *CRAP*, as it prefers to be known, is an eclectic ezine with loose filmatic themes and now it's turned its hands to TV as well.

Defenestrate   **www3.bc.sympatico.ca/defenestrate**
Humour from an engineering student? Stranger things have happened. Inspiringly named after one of the best words in the English language.

Disgruntled Housewife   **www.disgruntledhousewife.com**
A guide to modern living and intersex relationships. The dick list, meals men like, dirty secrets and 'Ask Queenie' all make essential reading for the modern girl.

Dog Butt   www.dogbutt.com

Tasteless humour ezine. Low points include postcards of deformed babies, 'Mighty Morphin' Mongoloids' (morph politicians into . . .) and hints for Japanese visiting the US.

The Drudge Report   www.drudgereport.com

Political rumour and news from Matt Drudge. Very hit-and-miss on the factual front but with a huge web following. After all, this is the site that broke Lewinskygate.

Emporium of Fruit   www.emporiumoffruit.co.uk

UK humour zine. Report sightings of Britain's finest TV presenter through the Chegwin alert, hear the absurd movie pitch of the day and brighten up your PC with desktop hell.

Fade to Black   www.fadetoblack.com

The same sort of idea as *The Onion* (see below). High points include the Hollywood executive quote of the day, unintentionally funny site of the day, sweating for Christ, Death Row inmates as film critics and hottest feminist competition.

Fitshaced   www.fitshaced.com

Claims to be the angriest, most disgruntled magazine on the net. Not enough to stop them cashing in with their own range of merchandise.

Fleapit   www.fleapit.com

Swaggering with more bravado and self-importance than a young Muhammed Ali, *Fleapit* is dedicating itself to asking the questions that other ezine creators wouldn't dare think about. After the flaying delivered to Simon Le Bon, down-at-heel eighties icons may think before opening their traps, but maybe A-ha should be left out in their obscure hinterland.

Fuck Everything Zine   www.fezine.com

Grrrr! Really angry, they hate everything. Adolescent angst outlet for the 'You hate me' generation.

Gorilla, Gorilla, Gorilla www.gorillagorillagorilla.com

If lurid lime-green ezines are your bag then fancies will be well and truly tickled at *Gorilla, Gorilla, Gorilla*. Find out if the rumours that mumbling is to be outlawed and that Fonzie has the key to the dwindling squid population are based on fact.

Grrl Ezine www.grrl.com/ebay.html

The strange world of Bonnie Burton. Absurd auction finds. For girls who missed out on all those kitsch 70s goodies in their teens, they can see that they didn't really miss anything at all.

Hobo Times www.hobo.org

There must be prizes for guessing why there's an official website for vagrants and freight train riders. *Hobo Times* is that organ, and it's going to take more than some Kerouac imagery to persuade the average tramp to swap his Super Brew for a laptop.

Inept www.inept.com

Dublin-based zine that claims to address the burning issues in modern culture. High points include 'What's Going On With Coleslaw?', a question that doesn't get asked every day.

The Journal of Mundane Behaviour www.mundanebehaviour.org

Exactly what it says it is. Anyone who thinks that their life is boring needs to pay a visit to plumb the depths of boring activities.

Lobster www.lobster-magazine.co.uk

The journal of parapolitics, intelligence and State Research, whatever that means. *Lobster* is edited and published by Robin Ramsay, who seems to know a lot of stuff that he shouldn't. A conspiracy Mecca.

Luke Ford www.lukeford.com

Offers unsubstantiated lurid stories and news items of employees in the porn industry. As fascinating as rubbernecking a car crash.

The Morning Star   www.poptel.org.uk/morning-star
The world's only Communist daily for those 'fed up with the propaganda of the capitalist giants or the false drama of the showbiz gossip'. Right on, kids.

Must Be Destroyed   www.mustbedestroyed.com
Where overhyped media creations get their comeuppance. Anyone who hates Pokémon or the Back Street Boys can get even without getting incarcerated. See Pokémon figures in various torture poses as well.

Octane   www.octanecreative.com
Home of the Duct Tape guys and Parodyville. The pig population doesn't get off so easy, and the Spam Bowling Arcade is lovingly sponsored by Spamdex Running Shorts.

The Onion   www.theonion.com
One of the most famous ezines. Absolutely recommended to anyone with a sense of humour, this is satirical humour at its best. With spin-offs into books, expect the TV series soon.

Positive Press   www.positivepress.com
An online version of the 'and finally . . .' bit from the news. With so much miserable, depressing news hitting our papers and screens every day it's easy to lose sight of the fact that lots of great things happen to people as well. *Positive Press* is a shiny, happy news site which is put together to show that the world isn't such a bad place after all.

Reuters Oddly Enough   http://news.excite.com/odd
A collection of wacky news stories from Reuters, so they must be true. Impress your friends with your knowledge of the bizarre.

Roadkill Quarterly   www.collideascope.com/rkq
If the scraping a partially rotted animal corpse off a roadside is your idea of preparing a meal then this is your recipe book. 'If it tastes too strong it's been dead too long'.

Shift-F7's Weird Wide Web
www.shift-f7.com

An ezine that relies heavily on an in-depth analysis of the musings of the top TV 'tec/pathologist Quincy. Superficially lightweight but highlights an interesting connection between overbathing and an untimely demise.

Smell the Coffee
www.smellthecoffee.com

Taking the whole business of being a coffee connoisseur a bit too seriously. A whole community of caffeine addicts wax lyrical on the merits of their favourite pick-me-up.

The Smoking Gun
www.thesmokinggun.com

Digging the dirt behind the headlines – cool, confidential and quirky. Get the real deal here.

Temple Ov Thee Leemur
http://totl.net

Humour that includes 'Instant Monkeys', 'Sell your Soul', 'The Beer Witch Project', potato-powered webservers and extreme cocoa.

Trailer Trash Monthly Combined With Redneck Quarterly
www.michaelchaney.com/trailertrash

Brimming with practical advice on keeping trespassers at bay and the fashionable ways of chewing tobacco wads, *Trailer Trash Monthly Combined With Redneck Quarterly* is resolutely aimed at individuals who breathe through their teeth and are overly fond of saying, 'You ain't from around these parts, are ya?' Hardly surprising that they're called rednecks when they're constantly looking over their shoulders for the next tornado.

Tuna Free Dolphin Meat
www.tunafree.com.au

Not ways of cooking up Flipper but a satirical ezine. The name is as attention-grabbing as the site intends to be.

Upright Citizens Brigade
www.uprightcitizens.org

The online world of this Comedy Central sketch troupe. A site as bizarre as the comedians themselves, which is so randomly put together that it takes a long while to work out what's going on.

Weekly World News   www.wwnonline.com

The logical conclusion to tabloid culture's quest for the lowest
common denominator of those of short attention span is the
Internet edition of the *Weekly World News*. Think that *Sunday
Sport* is a little far-fetched? Think again. This has all the usual alien
kidnappings, pneumatic sex kittens and even the 'outing' of Middle
Eastern dictators.

Wetlog   www.wrongwaygoback.com

Part of the Linksluts network. Random log of one person's life. A bit
like a perpetual soap opera or Bridget Jones gone mad.

Yo Mama   www.yomama.com

Loads of Yo Mama insults, T-shirts and postcards, and they can
even be delivered by email. The chances are that, if you're British,
this will mean nothing to you.

12//FOOD & DRINK

What better environment to share recipes and the joy of gastronomy than the web? The ultimate cookbook and restaurant guide.

Eating

Delve into the most amazing detail about common household foodstuffs and be amazed at food that most people didn't know existed. No more is waxing lyrical about food and drink the preserve of TV chefs with overinflated wallets and egos. Now anyone with a PC can share their loves and hates with other foodies.

All About Cheese   **www.cheese.com**
Exactly what it says. A database of nearly 700 varieties, compiling most of the world's knowledge of the best use for rancid milk.

The Bacon Worship Page   **www.captaincanada.com/bacon**
Even the hardest-core veggie would be loath to admit that they don't get a bit dewy-eyed when confronted by the whiff of a bacon sarnie. This site is a homage for the hardened carnivore with a thing for pig meat.

Cooking With   **www.NeoSoft.com/stealth/**
Cat Food   **catfood/front_m.html**
Now that new students are safely ensconced at their colleges, the first cases of malnutrition are probably beginning to set in. Well, Big Bad Bob can probably help them with an entire site devoted to gastronomical applications of feline nutrients. A must for all impoverished academic types who've graduated from dog biscuits.

Edible Insects   **www.eatbug.com**
There's a good reason why people don't eat insects: they're horrible, and warm-blooded animals are a far tastier bet. Being able to read these horrible thoughts via the web means the chances of

insect eating being a necessity are almost negligible, but it's a great way to feel superior.

Elvis's Wonderful   www.geocities.com/
World of Cheese   Hollywood/Mansion/5028
A foul testament to all things lacking in taste. One man's mission to declare war on some of the more tacky things that reside in our modern world. From Vegas to polyester leisure suits, nothing is safe.

Final Meal Requests   www.tdcj.state.tx.us/stat/finalmeals.htm
Like, it's going to be any consolation for your imminently premature demise. The tradition of offering condemned prisoners the choice of a last meal has been immortalised for the world to see, unlike the victims. This fascinatingly macabre meal collection is all cheerfully put together by those caring types at the Texas Department of Criminal Justice.

Gourmet Recipes for   www.geocities.com/
the Culinary Challenged   NapaValley/Cellar/3517
A unique take on the culinary arts. Particularly useful for the party monster, in need of stodge, is Death Warmed Up, which we are told is 'best enjoyed accompanied by strong hangover'. Which basically involves taking all the leftovers from the night before and cooking them up. Best of all is Janet's Double D Ambrosia Cups, which requires a bra and no kitchen utensils or pots to mould a pudding.

The Greaser   www.cantrell.org.uk/david/greaser
Everyone knows that the best hangover cure is a quick trip to the local greasy spoon. If the unreasonable commitments of a work timetable prevent this, then a trip to Dave and Gav's Greasy Spoon will get the morning-after victim salivating. For those too paralysed with pain to leave their desk, relief can be found at the Virtual Café, which allows the user to construct their own plate of lard-based tucker. A regular patron/victim, Karl Marx, says, ''Ealthy eating ain't what it used to be.'

The Hungover   **www.dantenet.com/**
Gourmet   **hungover/hungover.html**

A collection of recipes and cocktails aimed squarely at the modern man whose cooking repertoire stops at incinerating a few barbecue burgers. Cooking will never be a sissy hobby again, as heaps of men start fantasising about being Marco Pierre White and create new atrocities in their kitchens.

Jaffa Cakes' website   **www.jaffacakes.co.uk**

The nation's favourite biscuit addiction has made it to cyberspace for office workers to have a quick fix without all the associated calories.

Jesus Was a Vegetarian   **www.jesusveg.com**

Even the most liberal interpretation of the Bible goes off at a bit of a tangent for this one. If some religious zealot claimed the Son of God was a road drill there'd probably be a bit of text to support it. So here it is: the Saviour was a tree-hugging hippie – well, after all, he did have long hair and a beard.

Kitty Litter   **http://members.tripod.com/**
Cake   **~MemphisJan/litter.html**

Taking pet ownership many steps too far is this foul recipe. Closer inspection reveals that it's not quite as bad as it seems, as it's a perfectly edible cake that's served up in a litter tray with a dubious-looking smattering of chocolate lumps. All beautifully served up in a pooper scooper. Yuk!

The last dinner on   **www.armchair.com/**
the *Titanic*   **recipe/titanic1.html**

Could well be the second most famous meal after the Last Supper. When the *Titanic* disappeared to the bottom of the Atlantic in 1912 its first-class passengers, who had paid the equivalent of over £80,000 for their trip, had just finished their splendid ten-course meal. This site lists the menu of this particular last supper.

Leonard Nimoy Should Eat   http://web.tampabay.rr.com/
More Salsa Foundation   **lnsemsf**
The aftermath of a collision between *Star Trek* and gastronomy.
Graphic proof of why the pointy-eared chap from the cult TV show
should chew down on more salsa. Apparently if he had done this he
would have become 'an unstoppable force of excellence', an
argument that will probably rage at science-fiction conventions for
many years to come.

A Moron's Guide to Toast www.geocities.com/toastformorons
All the information that anyone needs for getting the most out of
this student staple.

101 Testicle Recipes & Fun Facts **www.funlinked.com/testicle**
Quite why the Canadian girl responsible for this collection of
unusual recipes put them on the web could probably fill a
psychology dissertation, but here they are. Men from all over the
world will wince as they very rapidly glance over these pages; but
women will probably love to remind them of it.

Penguin Caffeinated Peppermints **www.peppermints.com**
To climb to the top of the corporate ladder you have to be on the
go 24 hours a day. When one time-poor exec noticed how many
times he was chucking down an espresso and then popping a mint
into his mouth before meetings he came up with a time-saving
idea. Having combined the caffeine buzz and the fresh breath into
one package, he left his company to market these.

Planet Ketchup   **www.ketchup.wonderland.org**
Apparently ketchup is the king of condiments and can be found in
over 97 per cent of All-American kitchens. Planet Ketchup is
dedicated to people who really love the stuff and squirt it on
everything. Be amazed.

The Possum Cookbook
www2.msstate.edu/ ~brb1/possum.html

Not recommended for lovers of cute fluffy animals, or for vegetarians. The diverse recipes include Possum Creole, Possum Stew, Cajun Possum Chilli and Possum Tartare. Bearing in mind that most supermarkets haven't started selling them yet, there's also some useful advice on catching your dinner.

Ray's List of Weird and Disgusting Foods
www.andreas.com/ ray/food.html

Food to avoid at all costs if Sardinian maggot cheese, Mexican moles or Canadian seal-flipper pies don't appeal. Everyone's got their pet hates but most of them probably don't come close to these gastronomic monstrosities. Best avoided after a hearty meal.

Red Meat
www.redmeat.com

A bit of a red herring, this one, and strangely enough has nothing to do with food at all. It's actually the site to showcase Max Cannon's cartoon strips but, with sections such as 'Meat Locker', 'Meat Wagon' and 'Fresh Meat', people can be forgiven for being confused.

Redneck Sushi
www.magiclink.com/web/redneck

No, it's not a hillbilly delicacy comprising road kill: it's actually the brand name for a series of trout-based products from the Deep South of America. From the common 'Bubba' to the slightly more dignified 'Thurston Howell III', it's a class above most redneck cuisine.

Stim U Gum
www.offcolor.com/gum1.htm

Coffee that doesn't spill, for those hairy moments when the last thing that anyone wants to be wearing is their cappuccino. Caffeine-enhanced chewing gum could well be the thing for those mega road trips.

Street Food Around the World

www.openair.org/opair/strtfood.html

Beer, then kebab, football and hotdogs – the site that won't let gastronomic snobs forget about the bounteous food of the pavement. Even resorting to poems about food, the whole thing is garnished with links to every street food site known.

Top Secret Recipes

www.topsecretrecipes.com

All the top restaurants and fast-food megacorporations make sure that nobody finds out the secret to their recipes. Until now, that is. This whistle-blowing site is spilling the beans on some of the darkest-held secrets of McDonald's and Hard Rock Cafés. Worth a visit to finally find out what you're paying your money for.

2 Eggs, Sausage, Beans, Tomatoes, 2 Toast, Large Tea, Cheerslove

www.angelfire.com/ok/cheerslove

If you're not a morning person or you've just got a hangover that can be cured only by shovelling a large quantity of lard down your throat, then this will help with all your morning dietary needs. Recipes, eateries, suggested conversation and even breakfast jokes all stop you having to think before lunchtime.

Virtual Omelette

http://source.syr.edu/OS_omelette

Why send an electronic birthday card to a loved one when you can send them a picture of an omelette cooked to your own specifications? Then again, why would anyone want to send an omelette to anyone? Doesn't everyone prefer pizzas?

Weird Recipes

www.twics.com/~sabu/roadkill.html

Leah Smith collects oddball recipes. What she means by oddball is 'the recipes you serve but don't reveal, because their ingredients and simplicity embarrass you'. Find out what she means and suggest some more.

Drinking

From wine critics to outdoor lager enthusiasts, the joys of boozing have captivated man throughout history. It's not just alcoholic beverages that people pay tribute to on the web: there are plenty of other drinks that are at the top of people's favourites lists.

Bong Water www.bevnet.com/reviews/bongwater/index.asp
Obviously designed to catch out unsuspecting hippies, this is a truly pointless beverage. First of all, they brewed beer and then they took out the alcohol and yeast and anything that would make people buy it. Apparently, it's very healthy, but so is water, and that's cheaper.

Drunk of the Month www.iamdrunk.com
Public opinion seems pretty unanimous on the subject – it's not big and it's not clever, but most people still do it. Drink, that is. As if a skull-splitting hangover weren't enough of a punishment, seeing your most undignified moment glorified in Drunk of the Month might encourage a few people to take up more genteel leisure pursuits.

The Evils of Tea www.quite.com/
(and the Virtues of Beer) misc/tea1.htm
Find out once and for all which is better. So completely biased towards the cold brown stuff that there's not a single rational argument. The modern drunkard can arm themselves with such a plethora of pro-beer facts that anyone accusing them of being drunk will be overcome with the shame of their own ignorance.

Extreme Coffee www.shockalots.com
After extreme sports this is a drink truly worthy of the title. It's hyper-caffeinated coffee naturally loaded with more than 50 per cent more caffeine than your average brew. The company claims that it contains 'about 200mg of heart-pounding caffeine per 6oz cup or 2oz espresso shot', and after delivering a health warning

adds, 'Why Shock? Because sleep is overrated.' Buzz until dawn –
and then some.

The Global Hangover Guide   www.hangoverguide.com
The good server for all drinking classes. Telling you the best places
to get your hangover and the best ways to deal with it.

Happy Drunks   www.happydrunks.com
Dedicated to all things bacchanalian, Happy Drunks is the other
place to visit after closing time. Find out how 'Beer Goggles' affects
your vision and taste, whether you make the 'Hall of Ugliness',
whether you're a happy drunk – and if it all proves a little traumatic
then seek advice from Wino, the resident agony uncle.

Have a Brew   www.have-a-brew.com
Who can argue with a catchphrase like this: 'Man + beer = more
man'? Well, plenty of people can, but none of the regulars at Have
a Brew. With an online beer store and the unique 'Find Some Beer',
the all-beer search engine catering for all beer-related links, there's
no more that a beer enthusiast could want that doesn't come in a
glass.

Hot Rod Magazine   www.bevnet.com/reviews/
sodas   hotrod/index.asp
Those hard-living fifties types at *Hot Rod* magazine decided to
launch their own brand of driving-friendly beverages. They came up
with some unique produce names including Stroked & Bored
Strawberry Soda and Nitrous Orange Soda.

I Drink   www.idrink.com
The world's premiere resource with over 5,000 drink recipes and
cocktails. A must for the upmarket alcoholic who can't quite
stomach a can of Special Brew.

Mr T's Wine Reviews   www.webvs.com/wineview/mr.htm
Not the most obvious choice for a bacchanalian critic. This site is
such a disappointment with an impostor luring people under false

pretences. No 'cane that Chardonnay, sucka' here, just wholesome advice.

Shaken Not Stirred   www.martinis.com

The self-proclaimed Pit Stop on the Road to Perdition, where all things pertaining to Bond's favourite liquid refreshment are discussed alongside a directory of suggested places to gulp one down.

Sob'r-K   www.hangoverstopper.com

A product that claims to combat the adverse effects of alcohol. With litigation what it is in the States, there could be a few bucks to be earned by knocking back a bottle of absinthe, getting a medical certificate saying you've got a hangover and then suing their lying asses.

Starbucked   www.starbucked.com

A hapless punter called Jeremy Dorosin bought a coffee machine from Starbucks which didn't work, and when he tried to take it back he was so horrified by their customer service that he decided to get even by telling the world about his treatment. So he set up this website and started collecting letters from other disgruntled customers around the world.

A world of tea   www.stashtea.com

Visitors to the UK who catch the odd episode of *EastEnders* might be forgiven for thinking that most of today's ailments can be made better with a nice cup of tea. From bereavement to dismemberment, they're all fine after a quick cuppa, such is the nation's passion for the best drink of the day. Find out all the history, cultural significance and ways of making the nation's favourite drink.

13//HOBBIES & LIFESTYLES

Things that you do for fun when you don't have to do things that you have to do. The sheer range of hobbies available to while away the hours is a real testament to mankind's imagination. To an outsider they can seem bafflingly strange and pointless, but to the devotee they can become a way of life.

Alternative ways of living

The web is a great meeting place. No longer will people with so-called peculiar outlooks on life be consigned to the social outcast bin. Find out that you're not as weird as you thought with these sites.

British Naturism　　　　　　**www.british-naturism.org.uk**
The UK certainly isn't the best climate if naturism is your bag. Those who bravely pursue nude table tennis and supermarket shopping will find most of their needs catered for here. Including a directory of nudie beaches for wrinkly old men to parade their wares on.

Dangerous Jobs List　　**www.fieldingtravel.com/df/dngrjobs.htm**
Wage slavery sapping your will to live? Count your blessings if your profession isn't included in the Dangerous Jobs List and indulge in some quality daydreaming.

Dirty Sole Society　　　　　　　　**www.barefooters.org**
Shoes were invented for a reason: they stop your feet getting cold or pierced by sharp objects, and stop you ever having to feel dog turds. This group of people have regressed to their inner Sandy Shaws and are making a lifestyle out of being timid, partial naturists from the ankle down.

Eco Village Information Service www.gaia.org
A bit like *The Good Life* on a grand scale. Sponsored by the Danish Gaia Trust, this huge site is part of (obviously) an international collaboration whose mission is to spread news and help people who want to start living off the land and stop being so much like Margot.

International Vampire www.xs4all.nl/~intrvamp/main.htm
It's entirely forgivable to labour under the misapprehension that vampires communicate by swapping ectoplasm and other bodily secretions. Today's modern ghoul wouldn't be seen alive using such archaic methods: they'd be logged into International Vampire. The fact that it's hosted by a bank clerk will be no surprise to those who think that all financial institutions are manned by blood-sucking leeches.

National Caravan Council www.martex.co.uk/ncc
Opinion is polarised by these houses on wheels. Nirvana if you're committed to causing ten-mile traffic jams or want to know where to go and slash their tyres.

Panhandling Effectiveness http://charity.artificial.com/
Survey survey/
With more people than ever falling down on their luck and ending up living on the streets, spending a bit of time here could be one of the best career investments available. This interactive test allows you to test the effectiveness of seven actual working panhandlers in New York.

Pimp Daddy www.pimpdaddy.com
Pimping, the world's second-oldest profession. Learn how to dress like a pavement prima donna, send postcards and learn sharp insults from hundreds of Yo Mama … snaps.

You really must get out more

Dismal entertainment for the imagination-deficient out there. Don't try these at home.

Blackout's Box
www.blackout.com

A phone prankster boasts of his past achievements in a fully media-laden site. People who don't find this thing in the slightest bit funny could always go around to his house and burn it down. After all, prevention is better than cure.

Durham University Fart Lighting Society
http://members.tripod.com/~DUFLS

Another example of why people hate students. Not only do they rejoice in the fact that they've mastered the devilishly hard trick of lighting their own farts, but they've formed a club that even has its own website with an Italian version. Potential employers should remember never to interview any of them.

The First Sugar Packet Club in the UK
http://web.ukonline.co.uk/email.ukscsugar

There's a point at which collecting things jumps from being an innocent hobby to a strange obsession. Questions need to be asked if you find yourself collecting sugar sachets and these are the people to ask.

Groupie Central
www.groupiecentral.com

There's a name for girls who think nothing of blowing off a bouncer as a way to get close and personal with their favourite band members – and that name is groupie. From aspiring to retired groupies, this is the fount of all music-related carnal knowledge.

Home Canning Online
www.home-canning.com

Essential reading for jumble-salers and white supremacists. How to do it, what with, but not why.

Latrinalia   www.latrinalia.com

Latrinalia: the study of restroom graffiti. Which is fine if hanging around public toilets is your bag. How embarrassing for the intellectual with a genuine interest to explain to their boss exactly why they were arrested in their local conveniences at the weekend.

National Search for the Silliest   www.sillyputty.com/
Uses for Silly Putty   silly_contest/silly_contest.htm

Silly putty is like Plasticine with added bounce. A bizarre combination in one toy and obviously a concept from the drug-addled seventies. Anyone who's ever spared a thought about it since childhood can share it with other like-minded individuals.

Peanut Butter Lovers' Club   www.peanutbutterlovers.com

One person in two hundred people is fatally allergic to peanuts. For any of the other 199 with a passion there's a club for one of the world's favourite foods. Apparently, peanut butter is a staple in three-quarters of American households. After all, if it was good enough for the King . . .

Plaster of Paradise   http://castroom.com/pop

If the sight of people wearing plaster casts does strange things to you then don't panic: you're not alone. This site is dedicated to 'casters' throughout the world, so, if the world's looked different ever since you fell over drunk that time, visit this site to be among friends.

SKS buyback program   www.sksbuyback.org

Reformed psychopaths can now earn themselves $230 if they happen to live in California. Enthusiastic amateur murderers who can't get a decent part-exchange price for a weapons upgrade now know where to go.

Slaw Slam 2000   www.fluffybunnys.com/slaw.html

A firm favourite of biker rallies. When jelly and mud wrestling is just too low-calorie for the big mommas of the wrestling world they choose their favourite fighting environment, coleslaw. Good clean American fun, with added vitamins.

Sniper Country   www.snipercountry.com
For all your lone gunman needs. Most people's needs are 'Please go away and practise on yourselves, you freaks!' The perfect boutique for society's disenfranchised to tool up and create some headlines.

Spicy Food in your Pants   http://go.to/tinglingbits
A truly specialised and smelly fetish. There are people who like to put burning, chilli-laden foodstuffs down the front of their pants. They're not even doing it to appear in the Japanese game show *Endurance* or for a bet. Find out what the best dishes are to get your smalls steaming.

The Stinky Feet Project   www.ontap.com
Find out what happens when one man decides to infect himself with the athlete's-foot fungus (*Trichophyton mentagrophytes)* and the stinking aftermath in his daily diary.

The Stinky Meat Project   www.stinkymeat.net
The fully illustrated story of nineteen days' worth of one man's persecution of his neighbour in the name of science. This strange individual lobbed a load of meat over his garden fence into a secluded spot and documented the resulting decay. He finishes off with 'Fortunately, I wasn't arrested – so I am free to do it all over again.' Pray he doesn't move next door.

The Universe of Bagpipes   www.mcn.org/2/oseeler/bagpipes
What manner of aural hell could leave people begging for the latest teenie chart sensation? Look no further than the most derided instrument of all time. Every type of bagpipe, and even the hurdy gurdy, is examined in microscopic detail, explaining the full horror of these dreadful windbags. To cap it all, there's an opportunity to buy a CD featuring thirty types of 'pipe'.

Save it for a rainy day

Bizarre things to try when you're truly at the end of your tether.

Cigar Life   www.cigarlife.com
What do Sharon Stone, Demi Moore and Madonna all have in common? Apart from wads of cash and dubious acting ability, they've all bought into America's latest craze. If paying hundreds of pounds to set fire to a few mouldy leaves rolled on the thighs of Havana's finest virgins is your idea of sophistication, or indeed the cutting edge of feminist ideology, then this is your mag.

The Contortion Homepage   www.contortionhomepage.com
If we'd been meant to tie ourselves into knots we would have surely been born with bendy bones. The folk at Crystal Lizard Studios are trying to show to the world that putting your feet behind your ears is not the sole preserve of the porn industry.

Fume in a New York Traffic Jam   www.ny-taxi.com
Clever da Silva is fully wired in his NY taxi. Although why on Earth anybody would want to listen to a cabbie's inane rambling without even going anywhere is a bit of a mystery. Still, if his website takes off he'll never have to drive again.

Hot Wheels   www.hotwheels.com
Spending all your money on your motor? Ever wondered where this obsession came from? You can probably trace it back to childhood and exposure to these toys, which are the equivalent of motoring crack. Tiny little cars that would zip across the kitchen floor, bugging parents and causing havoc. This site will bring the memories flooding back.

The Imp Site   http://users.bart.nl/~franka/imps.html
People, usually men, do get very attached to their cars. The Hillman Imp is a little oddity that, despite its size, rear engine, and leaky windows, seems to have charmed a generation of owners from the

seventies so that an estimated 20,000 survive today. This site is a homage to the cute little thing with all the information that owners are ever likely to need.

Makeover www.futile.com/makeover
Send a photograph of yourself and the team at futile.com promise to turn you into a 'hypnotic mutant beauty'. Obviously nobody's going to do this, so how about humiliating your friends? Celebrity makeovers are predictably cheap shots.

Mountain IQ www.abbeyinn.com/html/mountain_i.q..html
Rambling Pac-A-Mac types can avoid the wrath of mountain-rescue types by never leaving home without a fair idea of their Mountain IQ. Then again it is the cheapest way of getting a ride in a helicopter.

Phonebashing www.phonebashing.com
Just when it seemed that people were grudgingly learning to accept that the mobile phone is going to become a way of modern living, a small pocket of resistance springs up. Dressed up as cellphones, they grab mobiles from people and stamp on them. All lovingly filmed for our viewing pleasure.

Professional & Executive Motorcyclists' Club www.pemc.co.uk
It's a sure sign that the male menopause has struck when the boss walks into the office looking like something out of *Easy Rider*. Point him in the direction of this group of middle-aged baldies so that he's got company when he wobbles off towards the suburban sunset on his brand-new Harley to the rousing refrains of 'Born To Be Wild'.

Shopping Cart Abuse www.shoppingcartabuse.com
There's nothing more predictable than the ensuing merriment when a load of drunk students happen upon an abandoned shopping trolley. It's even worse when, in the cold light of day, they boast about their antics by way of their own website.

The Tombstone Tourist www.teleport.com/~stanton

For sightseeing with a bizarre twist, how about checking out some famous burial sites? One man's hobby is documented with a list of all his favourite sightings, including Jimi Hendrix, John Belushi, Blind Lemon Jefferson and Roy Orbison.

The Wedgie www.geocities.com/Heartland/
Page Prairie/9179/wedgie.htm

Schoolyard embarrassment lives for ever. Targeting a truly unique and demographic group by claiming that the page celebrates 'the time-honoured hiking of another boy's underwear up his butt crack for humiliation in front of others in the 9 to 14 age group'.

World Nettle Eating Championship www.nettleeating.co.uk

Extreme sport or downright drunken hick stupidity? The Bottle Inn has been hosting an annual nettle-eating competition for a number of years. Find out where and when. Presumably the whole night is rounded off with fart lighting and shopping-trolley racing.

14//LANGUAGE

The web is often knocked as one of the evil tools of globalisation, stripping communities of their identity and making the world a bland place. What these negative types seem to forget is that small pockets of people are striving to keep soon-to-be-forgotten languages and dialects alive. It's become an invaluable aid in keeping up with pretentious friends and making sure that you're always going to have the last say with a cunningly crafted sentence to knock 'em dead.

Fun with language

The joy of a living language is that it never stays the same. Come back from holiday and the whole country can be talking a strange new tongue. Keep up with the latest fads with the following selection of language-based sites.

American Ballet Theater's   **www.abt.org/**
Online Dictionary   **dictionary**
For those who don't know their *arrière* from their elevation, this handy little dictionary should prevent red faces at Sadler's Wells. No explanations for what the men put down the front of their tights, though.

Aphorisms Galore   **www.aphorismsgalore.com**
If you can't slay 'em dead with your razor-sharp wit, then use someone else's. This is a selection of classic quotes and witticisms to make sure that you always assert your intellectual superiority.

A.Word.A.Day   **www.wordsmith.org/words/today.html**
Gently expand your vocabulary daily. Don't be surprised when people look at you as if you've lost the plot when strings of incomprehensible babble flow from your mouth.

Bond Girl Name — www.dvd.com/stories/play/BondGirls

Just as most guys in a tux think they're 007, there can't be many gals who haven't fantasised about being that most glamorous of accessories, a Bond girl. Where do they get those painfully politically incorrect names from? The search is over: just type in your name to start your new life.

Conversational Terrorism — www.vandruff.com/art_converse.html

Highbrow retorts guaranteed to be the last word in a verbal battle. No more will you kick yourself for not being able to come up with a knock-'em-dead witticism, because you can learn a few trusty favourites here.

The Crude Thesaurus — http://khopesh.iwarp.com/crude.html

A great resource for all the euphemisms commonly associated with the human body and its activities. Proving that swearing is no substitute for a limited vocabulary.

Funny Name Server — http://funnyname.com

When looking up a company name in a phone book it's hard to stop the eye wandering to the more unusual names. The Funny Name Server is a repository for daft company names. With new websites popping up daily, this is one site that's never going to run out of material.

The Gallery of 'Misused' Quotation Marks — www.juvalamu.com/qmarks

Pernickety collection of badly spelled signs, with errant speech marks. A form of highbrow trainspotting.

Ka-BOOM! — www.geocities.com/Athens/Marathon/5150/dictionary

There are some words that are never going to make it to the Oxford or Webster's. Take, for example, comic-book sounds. This list is a collection of unique action noises with an explanation of the meaning and context of each.

The Klingon Language Institute   www.kli.org
Trekkies are renowned, and much derided, for getting a little too deep into their utopian space-travel fantasy. This lot are so deep down that there's no hope of a rescue. After liking the sound of the language spoken by the bad-boy Klingons, they've decided to try to make it really live with translations of the Bible and Shakespeare. It's probably best never to be collared by anyone boasting of their prowess for a language that they've invented from a TV show.

Lost in the   http://hearsay.simplenet.com/
Translation   translation
The next time a YTS translator renders a foreign art-house film unwatchable, take solace in the fact that choice phrases are probably wending their way to Lost in the Translation, placing particular emphasis on Hong Kong films ('How can you use my intestines as a gift?') and the world of advertising (KFC went from 'Finger Lickin' Good' to 'Eat your fingers off') it makes a fairly strong case for Esperanto.

Motherly   http://dearmom.infospace.com/
Reminders   Momtalk.htm
For those missing their maternal influence, Motherly Reminders will provide a healthy dose of nostalgia with lists of all those mumisms. 'Would you do that at home?' and 'You'll have your eye out' etc.

Operas and Composers –   http://gray.music.rhodes.edu/
A Pronunciation Guide   operahtmls/Wsounds/bizz.aiff
For people with aspirations to Frasier-esque levels of pomposity, this is the guide that will help them hold their own at dinner parties.

Plumbdesign   www.plumbdesign.com/thesaurus
Strange 3D thesaurus where words float in midair but are connected to their relations by thin lines. Very strange and stylish.

Prose as Deadly Torture   www.duke.edu/~saw1/stories.html
Cringeworthy stories to bring forth groans from their concluding
puns. A collection of tales culminating in a mangling of a well-
known phrase. The authors invite contributions for new punchlines.
Put them out of their misery: don't send them.

The Rap Dictionary   www.rapdict.org
Gangster-rap phraseology explained. An invaluable aid for struggling
dads trying to communicate with their hipster kids. Actually,
wannabe cool fathers should probably not attempt any of this if they
want to avoid being laughed at.

Roger's   www.viz.co.uk/profanisaurus/
Profanisaurus   profanis.htm
Puerile fun with *Viz*'s Roger Mellie character, who splutters
expletives at every opportunity. Impress new friends with your
swearing prowess.

The Skeptic's Dictionary   http://skepdic.com
Over three hundred sceptical definitions and essays on occult,
paranormal, supernatural and pseudoscientific ideas and practices.
A great starting point for the amateur conspiracy theorist.

Swear   www.geocities.com/SunsetStrip/
Page   Frontrow/1304/fuk.html
If you're not worried about a diminishing vocabulary and you think
swearing is big and clever but just don't get enough opportunities
to practise, then this is the place. While away the hours by hitting
the individual swear buttons to be rewarded with an obscenity.
String them together and a sure-fire case of Tourette's is imminent.

What a Load of   www.wmin.ac.uk/~sfgva/
Codswallop, Pet   ukus/ukus_noframe.html
If you get funny looks when you ask Americans for a fag or look
perplexed when they tell you that they're 'really pissed', then you
may need this dictionary of Anglo-American confusions. All those

strange little words and phrases that don't quite cross the Atlantic intact.

Word Perfect   **www.chisenhale.org.uk/ch2**
Not many people have noticed this. As software becomes more sophisticated everybody is typing up documents in the same few word-processing packages. As the spell checking and grammar functions 'improve' language is becoming universally sanitised and dehumanised. This site redresses the balance.

Word generators

With all the popularity of emails and web use, it's not hard to forget that computers are just that. They can perform enormously complex calculations. With so much information to take in it's hard to keep up with a living language, so there are a few websites that take the hard work out of being hip.

Automatic Complaint-Letter   **www-csag.cs.uiuc.edu/**
Generator   **individual/pakin/complaint**
Can't quite channel your rage into eloquent prose? This site takes all the hard work out of complaining with style.

Burn Me   **www.ontap.com/burn**
Convert meek text into a seething ball of hate.

Dialectizer   **http://rinkworks.com/dialect**
Brighten up boring websites by having them translated into a dialect of your choice. The Dialectizer will translate your favourite web pages into Redneck, Jive, Cockney, Elmer Fudd, Swedish Chef, Moron or Pig Latin. Could be one of the funniest sites on the whole Internet.

Glam Name   **http://qix.lm.com/cgi-bin/**
Generator   **fun/glamname.pl**
Get rid of that boring run-of-the-mill moniker by being a bit more *Ab Fab*. Alternative identities start with the input of your old label.

Meet Mr Insult!   **www.urban75.com/Mag/insult.html**

Really angry man, he hates everybody and everything. Anything you can insult he can do so much better. Give it your best shot: type in yours and watch him assert his authority.

Random Goth   **http://scribble.com/**
Lyric Generator   **dghq/gothlyric**

There's a certain familiarity about the lyrics produced by gothic bands. Not being able to face daylight can certainly reduce time for the creative process, so switch off the lights, log in and write a bestselling album. (See also 'Goths' in Chapter 4.)

The Surrealist   **www.madsci.org/cgi-bin/**
Compliment Generator   **cgiwrap/~lynn/jardin/SCG**

You are the swordfish that will never shower. Make your mark by complimenting people in such a strange way that they'll remember you for ever with this handy little gizmo. For the incurable romantic there are a few compliments in French too.

WuName   **www.recordstore.com/cgi-bin/wuname/wuname.pl**

The only chance mere mortals are going to get to join hip-hop's maddest, baddest gang. With this you get to find out what your name would translate into if you ever get asked to join the Wu Tang Clan.

15//LAW & ORDER

The criminal underworld is now firmly above ground with masses of sites devoted to crime, crimefighters and the results of crime.

The long arm of the law

Tirelessly fighting crime and getting stick from every direction, the boys and girls in blue have plenty of web presence.

The Absolute Worse Things   **www.geocities.com/Heartland/**
To Say To a Police Officer   **Prairie/7559/copjokes.html**
If home life's so bad that being locked up is preferable to domesticity, then this collection of lines is a dead cert to get you banged to rights.

Meet-An-Inmate.Com   **www.meet-an-inmate.com**
America's burgeoning prison population means that there are more and more people getting banged up for the most innocuous of crimes. If you're a do-gooder or all-round weirdo wanting to converse with female prisoners, then this site aims to put you in touch with some female villains.

Police Scanner   **www.policescanner.com**
Live a little dangerously from the comfort of your work desk. Eavesdrop on the emergency services via your PC. Waste hours of your time waiting for something interesting to happen while the police tootle around arresting shoplifters and jaywalkers.

Pursuit Watch   **www.pursuitwatch.com**
Americans need never miss the next high-profile cop chase. Next time OJ Simpson's trying to outgun the LAPD with the world's media in hot pursuit – and you're oblivious of the fact that you're missing the big sensationalist news story of the week – just

subscribe to this service. From the moment a police chase hits the TV screen you're told which channel to tune into via your pager.

The Sweeney   **www.thesweeney.com**

The undisputed Hardest Cops of the Seventies. Regan and Carter are back on TV and making their debut on the web at this official site. They would have told the nearest bird to go and put the kettle on while they shuffled around a dingy bedsit modelling the best in man-made fibres. Those not au fait with seventies Brit culture will need to study the 'Style Guide', which provides fascinating explanations of how only shirts with a high polyester content could give our heroes their authentic seventies underarm sweat patches. What is truly disappointing is the pitiful lack of cursing in each episode, as revealed by 'The Swearing Section'. All is redeemed in the sound-bites section, which allows visitors to hear Dennis Waterman saying 'Guvnor' ad infinitum.

A Treasury of   **http://members.aol.com/**
Police Humor   **GSPZ/policehumor.html**

The best example of an oxymoron on the web. Anyone who's ever heard those famous words, 'Good morning, Mr Schumacher, and you seem to have fallen down the stairs, sir', will be pleasantly surprised at this little collection. All those tiresome rozzer witticisms in one delectable package to ruin the surprise next time the long arm makes its presence felt.

Villains

It's always been cool to be a little bit dodgy but this lot might make people change their opinions.

Dumbcrooks   **www.dumbcrooks.com**

They usually get caught in the end. This is a collection of anecdotes about less than master criminals whose cards were marked the moment they walked out of their front doors.

Gang Land   **www.ganglandnews.com**
Jerry Capeci, America's foremost expert on organised crime, has compiled the world's most comprehensive website on the mob. Packed full of crime-boss bios and even a daily news service, this is a fascinating effort from a man who probably hasn't slept a wink in years.

Serial Killer Bureau www.apbnews.com/crimesolvers/serialkiller
A compendium of known serial-killer cases in the US. It includes web chats, features and daily news for those with an unhealthy attraction to the gruesome.

Banged to rights

Crime's a mug's game, make no mistake. Get caught and you'll be repenting at your leisure.

Corrupt Prison Guards   **www.prisoners.com/pubenem.html**
Pennsylvania State Cops have obviously upset the man behind this effort. Claiming that more of them are arrested for crimes than any other group of the same size, he's using the web to get even. By inviting people to share their experiences of the long arm of the law, he's managed to compile a list of alleged misdemeanours committed by corrupt state troopers.

Famous Mugshots   **www.mugshots.org**
When celebrities go off the rails and get banged up they have to endure the mugshot they know is going to be released to the press. Trying to live it down here are Hugh Grant, Jeffrey Dahmer and Pee Wee Herman.

Penpals Inside   **www.pennpals.org**
At the current rate that the US government is banging people up there are going to be more people inside than out. How are they going to find out what's going on outside? By a letter from a cheerful do-gooder that they've never met, that's how. For people

with a strange yearning to have a safe form of contact with their local serial killer, this is entirely risk-free.

Postcards From   **www.law.cam.ac.uk/users/**
Prison   **dep21/postcar2.htm**
Electronic postcards with a difference. Not for the 'Wish you were here . . .' types, these cards are all themed around the misery of incarceration. Best used to remind friends up to no good that they're going to get caught one day perhaps.

Women Behind Bars   **www.womenbehindbars.com**
Hard-working computer geeks have been using the net as a dating service for years. Those resorting to the contact point for female felons may find that they've been taking their work a little too seriously. Then again, they may consider that a mere $3 for four addresses and the thought of very cheap dates may let them save up for that new hard drive in their lives.

Justice will be served (eventually)

The law is a funny thing, best left to the professionals.

Citizen's Self-Arrest Form   **www.ou.edu/oupd/selfarr2.htm**
If you know you've committed a crime and you're waiting for that knock on the door, why waste good taxpayers' money by letting the police arrest you? Take this handy little form to your local cop shop and demand to be incarcerated. Literally saves hours of police processing time.

Crazy-Bitch   **www.crazy-bitch.com**
The owner of this site had an affair with his secretary. To say that his girlfriend went ballistic when she found out is to put it mildly – the understatement to beat all understatements. If a tornado had blown through his flat it would have done less damage. Examine the aftermath and help him decide whether he should have her put away.

Dumb Laws　　　　　　　　　　　　**www.dumblaws.com**
We've had our fair share of daft legislation recently, but we're mere amateurs compared with our American cousins – as this collection of staggeringly stupid rules from every state in the US will testify.

The Evidence Store　　　　　　　　**www.evidencestore.com**
A truly bizarre and specialised shopping experience, this service caters for lawyers needing courtroom props. This is the one-stop shop for people needing to rent human skeletons and other gruesome exhibits.

Rate Your Risk　　　　　　　　　**www.nashville.net/~police/risk**
Everyone's becoming more vulnerable to the threat of crime, but fortunately nobody's sure when it's going to happen to them. Become a paranoid, gibbering wreck by taking this test, which rates your chances of being raped, robbed, stabbed, shot, beaten, murdered or burgled. Happy viewing!

Ultimate auto theft　　　　　　　**http://cnn.com/WORLD/africa/**
deterrent　　　　　　　　　　　　**9812/11/flame.thrower.car**
The crime rate in South Africa is soaring out of control with car-jacks and armed robberies everyday occurrences. CNN reported on this story about a guy who wanted the ultimate theft deterrent fitted to his new set of wheels. At the touch of a button six-foot flames leap up the side of the car. With video demos thrown in, too.

Unclaimed Persons　　　　　　　　**http://170.164.50.2/**
List　　　　　　　　　　　　　　**coroner/IndigentList.asp**
This page contains a list of unclaimed persons throughout the United States and is maintained by the San Bernardino County Coroner's office. Not to be confused with unclaimed luggage departments at airports.

16//MAKING FRIENDS

There's more to the Internet than just passively reading from webpages or firing off the odd email. It's an interactive medium and at any given time there are countless people out there just dying for a bit of contact. From celebrity webchats to bulletin boards that will find the only other person in the world who shares your love of earwigs, there's an army of people out there who just want to make friends.

Usenet newsgroups

This is where the action happens. The highs and lows of the Internet. There are about five hundred different types of newsgroup but the alt (alternative) ones are the juicy flavours. Support and debate on every subject under the sun – and beyond. Unfortunately, it also plumbs the depths of human depravity. The web can't hold a candle to Usenet for filthy illegal sex, racism and violence, but only a tiny minority of its content is so foul. The rest is a global meeting place for the most special interests that the mind can handle. So, if you want to meet people who share your unique hunger for the bizarre, the following are places guaranteed to raise an eyebrow.

alt.aliens.they-are-here
They are, and Elvis works in a chip shop in Barnsley.

alt.amazon-women
Customers of online bookstore – or that Zena's got a lot to ask for.

alt.amusements-forsale.uk
Dodgem cars in the garden, anyone?

alt.angst
Everyone hates me. Not strictly true: the people who hang out here at least love each other.

alt.animals.zebu
Find out what a zebu is.

alt.backrubs
Lower . . . to the right . . . aaaah, that got it.

alt.bad-breath
Kissing-free zone. Someone suggest brushing their teeth and staying online.

alt.baldspot
Slapper support for the follicularly challenged.

alt.beer.like-molson-eh
Those Canadians do get a lot of flack, don't they?

alt.booger.misc
Nose goblins of the world unite.

alt.bugger-all
Not a thing, no.

alt.change.lightbulb
Find out how many people it really takes.

alt.complainers.bitch-n-moan
Have a whinge, you'll be in good company.

alt.cow.tipping
The sport of kings, and drunken students.

alt.dead.porn.stars
Plus the diseases that killed them.

alt.elvis.impersonators
Tips on how to get that rhinestone polished a treat. Join the union, get discount Brylcreem for life.

alt.flame.girlfriend
Whining little wusses bitch about the girls that they're too afraid of to dump.

alt.flame.jesus.christ
You've got to be brave to do this because the last flame doesn't belong to you.

alt.geek.supremacy
They shall truly inherit the Earth. Well possibly not, but their bank statements will have the last laugh.

alt.gothic.fashion
Isn't it all black? Sharpen those pointy boots.

alt.guinea.pig.conspiracy
Rodents are massing for the Great Rebellion.

alt.hangover
If you've got a hangover and you can negotiate a newsgroup then you haven't got a hangover.

alt.herpes.personals
People with herpes looking for companionship or a quickie.

alt.hilliterate.noarthern.bastards
Not perpetuating a stereotype or anything.

alt.is.bill.gates.satan
No he's just very rich. Satan's too cool to be a dweeb.

alt.marriage-minded.women
Run for the hills, boys. They're ganging up and they're coming to get you.

alt.out-of-body
Not out of your head.

alt.overweight.trailer-trash.jay-denebeim
The name says it all!

alt.pagan
You old witch. Meet some friends who'll let you dance naked in the woods with them.

alt.party.stag-night
Groom humiliation ideas.

alt.peanut-butter.electricity
A truly renewable energy source.

alt.penguin-fetish.recovery
Once they get you, you're in big trouble. So innocuous and they're only chocolate biscuits.

alt.recipes.babies
Another highly sustainable crop.

alt.redheads
Ginger support for coppertops.

alt.religion.drew-hamilton
Drew must be quite a guy.

alt.religion.druid
Beards, frogs and pointy hats. Plus the odd virgin sacrifice.

alt.religion.beavis-n-butthead
They make as much sense as the average evangelist.

alt.sex.nigelw.loves.sheep
Bet he doesn't any more. Now the whole world knows.

alt.shrinky.dinks
Remember them? Find out exactly what the point of them was.

alt.smouldering.frat.house
Spoiled brats finally did it.

alt.startrek.creative.erotica
Trekkie jazz matter. Erotica in the style of *Star Trek*. Meet the seedier devotees of sci-fi conventions.

alt.the-chaps
Exploits of the infamous Leeds Sharking Club.

alt.2eggs.sausage.beans.tomatoes.2toast.largetea.cheerslove
No black pudding, then?

alt.women.supremacy
Go Grrrls!

alt.y2k.end-of-the-world
Bet they feel stupid now.

Live chat

Find out too late that the person that you've been talking to for the last hour is actually a precocious nine-year-old. There are plenty of chat rooms out there. Go to Ask Jeeves and enquire where you can take part in a live chat and navigate to the discussion of your choice. An example of how diverse and specialist live chats can be found at: Internet Cigar Group's Cigar Chat Room (**www.cigargroup.com/Java/Ewgie/client**). Meet others who like to fill rooms with an aromatic fug and discuss how to stop your house smelling like a pub.

Just about every big website will host its own chat boards. Go to a search engine, find the topic you want and off you go. Yahoo.com has its own directory.

17//MOVIES

The magic of the silver screen never fails to captivate people's imaginations. The web is awash with tributes to films, actors, actresses, genres, review magazines, comedy magazines, and Mr T. All this and it's still the only way to get to see a trailer when you want to.

Movie reviews with a difference

While movie reviews are ten a penny on most movie sites, the following selection put a slightly more interesting spin on the art of film criticism.

Ain't It Cool News   **www.aint-it-cool-news.com**
Harry Knowles is a gargantuan, ginger film fanatic. When he started this insider gossip site he probably didn't know that he was going to become Hollywood's number-one enemy. Submissions from studio insiders have given the lowdown on some of the world's biggest films months before any righteous film critic gets to set eyes on it. He's been blamed for spilling the beans on loads of recent box office disasters and the site goes from strength to strength.

Blindside   **www.blindsidereviews.com**
Just because you're blind, it doesn't mean that you can't be A Movie Critic. This is the web home of the world's only blind movie critic.

Haiku Movie Reviews   **www.igs.net/~mtr/haiku-reviews.html**
Celluloid opinions in 5-7-5 syllables.

One Word Review   **www.fluffybunnys.com/reviews.html**
Expressing yourself in words is a truly venerable activity that people have been devoting their lives to for centuries. After all, the pen is mightier than the sword, and to be able to write a movie review that encapsulates your feelings in one word is to possess a truly remarkable weapon.

Rotten Tomatoes   **www.rottentomatoes.com**

A comprehensive reviews and previews publication with a unique rating system. All flicks are rated for their fresh/rotten tomato ratings.

Thugs On Film   **www.shockwave.com**

When it comes to TV film criticism, jumper-clad oldsters and hirsute boys with lisps can't cut the mustard when placed next to Cecil and Stubby, two East End lads with a healthy appreciation of the cinematic medium. Could well be the pinnacle of film criticism. Visit soon before it becomes a watered-down MTV slot.

About films

There are plenty of people who choose their own unique forms of film appreciation. Cataloguing continuity, nudity and clichés is just the start of it.

The Astounding B Monster   **www.bmonster.com**

There was a time before the Hollywood blockbuster when horror movies didn't have special effects. They cost 10 pence to make and suspension of disbelief, not CGI, was the order of the day. The generations brought up on these films had nowhere else to go. So, if you just can't resist films such as *The Mesa of Lost Women* and *The Hideous Sun Demon*, this is the place for you.

Austin Powers   **www.austinpowers.com**

The film website has become the essential weapon in the film marketeer's armoury. Unfortunately, they don't ever seem to be that bothered with making them interesting. Predictably formulaic, they seem to have become just another vehicle for showcasing the trailer. One exception to the rule is the Austin Powers site, which features sites for each of the films. Games, screensavers, wallpaper, pictures, sounds – in a word: shagadelic.

Celebrity Nude Database www.cndb.com
Built along the lines of the hallowed Internet Movie Database, this little gem aims to archive every clothesless scene on celluloid. Simply enter the name of your favourite lust objects into the search and relive some of those more personal moments. As yet unsponsored by a tissue company.

Dogme www.dogme95.dk
Dogme is a controversial new set of rules for filmmaking from Denmark. It's either the most pretentious, beret-wearing load of old guff or the breath of fresh air that's going to rejuvenate a stagnant film industry. Filmmakers must take the 'Vow of Chastity', which means getting back to grassroots filmmaking. Surprisingly the first few products have been really good.

Fake Movie Posters www.brutesquad.com
Pre-empting the mighty Hollywood studios, this dude designs them before the film's even been made. See Arnie as Oskar Schindler and Marlon Brando as Boss Hogg.

The Golden Raspberry Award Foundation www.razzies.com
While the Oscars celebrate all things fantastic in filmmaking, the Raspberries poke fun at all things rotten. They run at the same time as the Oscars, and the worst performances are jeered and laughed at. Having a Razzie will be a millstone around the neck of any career actor or actress.

Monster Home www.monsterhome.com/gray.htm
Second-rate, plotless, tragic sets with implausible characters in ridiculous costumes. In addition to all this, *Monster Home* claims to be the first film developed especially for the web. Had this kind of technology been available in the seventies, the world might have been spared the horror of Hammer.

Movie Mistakes   www.movie-mistakes.co.uk
If it doesn't make sense or shouldn't have happened, then it's probably been spotted and logged here.

The Movie Clichés List   www.moviecliches.com
'When you enjoy something, you must never let logic get too much in the way. Like the villains in all the James Bond movies. Whenever Bond breaks into the complex: "Ah, Mr Bond, welcome, come in. Let me show you my entire evil plan and then put you in a death machine that doesn't work." '

The Nitpickers Site   www.nitpickers.com
Another nightmare movie mistake site to haunt movie continuity people for the rest of their careers. Find out if you're the only person to notice the soldier wearing the digital watch in that medieval battle scene.

Ruining the Surprise   www.cinepad.com/
of Surprising Films   warning6.htm
Do you want to avoid having the surprise endings of over a hundred movies ruined for you? Then, for heaven's sake, don't click here!

Shark Attack   www.exposure.co.uk/eejit/3act/sharkattack.html
Budding directors can analyse a plot breakdown of one of Spielberg's masterpieces. Hats off for the patient types who've managed to re-enact *Jaws* entirely with their own Lego models.

Shock Cinema   http://members.aol.com/shockcin/main.html
If your appetite has been whetted for weird celluloid, then a visit to this site will bring any net sicko up to speed on sexploitation, blaxploitation, Mexploitation and Mondo.

South Park – The Movie   www.southparkmovie.com
The three games are what set it apart from traditional promo sites: 'Kick the Baby' (which involves hoofing Ike, Kyle's brother), 'Freedom Fighter' and 'Cartmangotchi' (feed that fat little git with cheesy puffs

until you piss him off enough to make him go home). Best mouse-over action anywhere.

Trailervision www.trailervision.com
Cinephiles with Attention Deficit Disorder whose boredom threshold won't let them make it through a whole feature will be captivated by this inspired idea. A compendium of trailers for films that don't even exist with titles that they wouldn't have dared use, even in the seventies.

Troma Studios www.troma.com
They make what would best be described as B-minus movies. They're responsible for *Tromeo and Juliet*, *Surf Nazis Must Die*, and *The Toxic Avenger*. They are Troma, and this is their world.

The name's Bond . . .

One of cinema's most enduring characters hasn't escaped the web experience.

Diana, Princess of Wales: www.mcs.net/~klast/
The Bond Connection www/diana.html
There are hundreds of James Bond sites but this page is one of the most bizarre. Consisting of a collection of photos of the late Princess of Wales meeting people connected with James Bond. Well collected, or something.

George Caroll's Cyber Salon www.georgecaroll.com/007.htm
A brief foray into the world of espionage for this Beverley Hills barber. Claiming that 'What all 007s had in common was great looking sexy hairstyles', he dissects their coiffeurs and gives practical tips on imitation.

The James Bond Formula www.sabram.com/site/bond.html
This spoilsport strips back the magic of the decades of Bond films to reveal that each film rigidly adheres to a common formula. The fact

that everyone knows this and doesn't seem to care hasn't deterred him.

Universal Exports www.universalexports.com
Every man in a tux thinks he looks like James Bond. Some of the guys who work aren't actually deluding themselves. This company operates themed events and lookalikes based on the never-ending action franchise.

That film with the light sabres

There's no film that can compete with the mighty Star Wars *franchise for webspace. With legions of fans who have either dedicated their lives to the movies or are secretly living the dream, it's no surprise that fans with only the slightest ability to code a web page have turned their hands to creating their own special form of homage.*

Alternate Casting http://www.blueharvest.net/cast
Just what if? What if Christopher Walken or Burt Reynolds had played Han Solo? John Travolta had been Luke Skywalker? For many the world would be a very different place. These are just some of the possibilities posed by the owner of this site.

Darth Maul Estrogen Brigade http://darthmauleb.cjb.net
Constructed by some of his more vociferous female fans. There's no arguing that he's definitely got the best weapon ever, and it's double-ended.

Darth Vader Crunched www.ionet.net/
My Balls ~wrightw/vader
Plenty of ball crunching and eating from *Star Wars* characters.

Diagnosing a www.hownowcow.com/
Redneck Jedi redneck.htm
If you've started to notice that your local Jedi is showing tendencies to drive a pickup truck and shoot beer cans, it could be worth

learning the best way of recognising him – before dispatching him to the great barn dance in the sky.

How To Make   **www.angelfire.com/la2/mdmlhp/**
Darth Maul's Lightsabre   **MakeDMaulsLightsaber.html**
Nerds! What exactly are you going to do with it? Impress your friends down the pub?

I Hate Star Wars   **www.ihatestarwars.com**
No, really, tell us what you actually think about the film. Set up to dampen the hype of one of the most eagerly awaited sequels of all time.

Jar Jar Binks   **www.geocities.com/BourbonStreet/**
Ate My Balls   **Canal/3538/binks.html**
How can a character who exists only in the RAM chips of a million special-effects computers evoke such hatred? Well the Prequel's own CGI-rendered Huggy Bear-alike Jar Jar Binks is that character.

Jar Jar Binks   **http://members.xoom.com/_XOOM/**
Must Die!   **scifimovies/news/jarjar.html**
Jar Jar didn't go down too well with established *Star Wars* fans. No sitting on the fence here.

Jar Jar Binks Must   **http://home.neo.rr.com/**
Fucking Die!   **dlr/antijj.htm**
Absolutely no room for doubt here. They don't like Jar Jar.

Mr T vs.   **www.geocities.com/SouthBeach/**
Darth Maul   **Cove/6155/tmaul1.html**
Wonder who wins? Lightsabres vs. mountains of tacky gold jewellery. There can be only one outcome …

The Phantom Menace   **http://web.nmsu.edu/~rtelles/**
Drinking Game   **tpmdrink.html**
Committed *Star Wars* fans and party revellers can see if they can make it to the end of the film before heading for the porcelain.

Save Jar Jar   www.abel-info.com/~twahlstrom/
Binks   savejarjarbinks/savejarjarbinks.html
Luckily, the web's always good for an alternative point of view.
Unfortunately, in spite of all the hard work that's gone into it, Jar
Jar is probably going to be woefully short on sympathisers.

Shaven Wookie   www.shavenwookie.com
Ever fantasised about a Wookie in the bath? Most people haven't
but there may be no depths to some people's obsessions, hence
this site. Also featured is '*Star Wars* meets *The Rocky Horror Picture
Show*', guaranteed to get people thrown out of cinemas and
potentially lynched the length of the land as people are encouraged
to scream out abuse at relevant points in the films.

Star Wars Asciimation   www.asciimation.co.nz
The daddy of all fan sites, which is utter geek nirvana. Bizarrely rude
ASCII pictures, made up of neatly arranged keyboard characters,
are a perennial office email favourite. This is a work of true devotion
started two years ago, and only now nearing completion in spite of
containing nearly 1,100 frames retelling the original saga.

Star Wars Stick Figures   www.infinityrealm.com/stick.html
For a truly minimalist take on character realisation, this is a
refreshingly original look at the series' favourite characters.

Trooper Clerks   www.studiocreations.com/trooperclerks
A movie short featuring a day in the life of a pair of storm troopers
gainfully employed in a convenience store. If it sounds uncannily
like a certain Kevin Smith film, then the sight of hockey-playing,
dancing troopers is proof positive.

Wookie Theatre!!   www.toshistation.com/wookie.htm
More *A-Team/Star Wars* frolics in with some unique takes on *Star
Wars* involvement in *The Dukes of Hazard*, *Blade Runner*, *Toy Story*
and *Alien*.

18//ORGANISATIONS

No self-respecting organisation would be without its own website nowadays – from the smallest museum to the biggest multinational corporation. It's a status symbol that has the advantage of telling people what you do and where you are.

The   **http://thecenter2000.com/**
Center 2000   **access_public_records.htm**
For American citizens only, for the time being. The Freedom of Information Act now lets Joe Citizen find out exactly what Uncle Sam has on him. Are you brave enough, punk? Well are you?

Pave the Planet Earth   **www.icbl.hw.ac.uk/**
with Asphalt   **~cjs/pave**
Not everyone agrees with tree-hugging, dungaree-wearing, cycling hippies that cars are a Bad Thing. There are some dedicated petrol heads out there who believe that the environmental impact of the car hasn't gone far enough and we should chop down all of the forests and pave the planet. Controversial stuff.

The Web's Smallest   **www.sylloge.com:8080/**
Art Museum   **5k/entries/82/a.html**
For the bandwidth-challenged art buff. A very skinny site with some predictably abstract exhibits including a few from Mondrian.

Museums

So most of the so-called museums on the web are dismal collections of tat amassed by weirdoes who want to shout about it. The curators of some of the world's more unique collections are embracing the web in an attempt to lure potential customers through their doors.

The American Diner Museum   **www.dinermuseum.org**
Fans of neon, waffles and bottomless coffees will soon have their
own Mecca in Rhode Island. Celebrating the nostalgic America of
the fifties, which probably never existed, this is sure to be a hit with
Japanese tourists.

Barney Smith's   **www.unusualmuseums.org/**
Toilet Seat Art Museum   **toilet**
Barney has been customising (and presumably using) toilet seats for
thirty years and he wants to share them. Now with over five
hundred exhibits.

The Bureau of Missing Socks   **www.funbureau.com**
The Bureau of Missing Socks is the first organisation solely devoted
to solving the question of what happens to missing single socks. It
explores all aspects of the phenomenon, including the occult,
conspiracy theories and extraterrestrials.

Cyberspace Vacuum   **www.137.com/museum/**
Cleaner Museum   **entrance.htm**
A tribute to the mighty domestic dust buster. A labour of love from
one dedicated enthusiast, confident that there are more like him
out there.

International Hamburger Hall of Fame   **www.burgerweb.com**
It's a travesty that the King, surely the most celebrated bacchanalian
since Henry VIII, never managed to visit the Burger Museum. At least
the world was spared the sight of the King astride a hamburger
Harley Davidson cruising the streets of Memphis in a rhinestone
jumpsuit.

Kooks Museum   **www.teleport.com/~dkossy**
The web has always been a cesspool for half-baked theories and
rants. It's not often that some of the more entertaining can be
found in one place, however. The Kooks Museum is exactly that: a
cornucopia of misguided thoughts from some of the planet's more

bonkers inhabitants. The more salubrious areas include the 'Library of Questionable Scholarship', 'Hall of Hate' and 'The Conspiracy Corridor'.

Museum of Menstruation and
Women's Health   www.mum.org
Its claim to be the only one of its kind in the world is no surprise to anyone. What is spectacularly baffling is the fact that its creator is a man. Why's he so interested?

Sulabh International
Museum of Toilets   www.sulabhtoiletmuseum.org
Spend a virtual penny at the Sulabh International Museum of Toilets. The bowels of this site contain a history of sanitation and the evolution of the common toilet.

Government departments

Governments are paying lip service to the web in an attempt to give the impression of being more accountable. Luckily there are a few interesting sites out there.

List of MI6 officers   http://jya.com/mi6-list.htm
There have been 35,000 requests and lots of press coverage for this page listing 'known' MI6 officers. Why any of this should mean anything to anybody is anyone's guess. But it's probably ruined a few long lunches in Whitehall.

Official CIA Website   www.odci.gov
Kennedy, Monroe, Bay of Pigs – read all about them here. Obviously not, since you're more likely to be traced and receive a visit from a door-kicking SWAT team in the middle of the night.

Official MI5 Website   **www.mi5.gov.uk**
All of Britain's best-kept secrets in one easy-to-navigate website.
Well, not really – just a simple corporate brochure which hopes to
recruit a few new spies.

Groups

*Why have a club newsletter when you can have a website and get
the added bonus of recruiting a few more members? The web is
now fully established as a virtual meeting point for all kinds of
like-minded individuals.*

Bad Breath Resource Centre   www.hhnews.com/badbreath.htm
Get your bad breath here! Chose your flavour for maximum impact.
OK, it's actually about ways to *prevent* halitosis.

Codpiece   www.teleport.com/~codpiece/
International   codpiece.shtml
This reeks of students obsessed with watching reruns of *Black
Adder*. The Codpiece Resurrection Society put their case for a
revival of this most curious menswear item.

The Dull Men's Club   www.dullmen.com
A place – in cyberspace – where Dull Men can share thoughts and
experiences, free from pressures to be 'in and trendy', to enjoy
instead the simple, ordinary things of everyday life. Visit and laugh at
them.

The 47 Society   www.47.net/47society
This group dedicate their efforts to this proudly random number.
The whole thing is way too highbrow for mere mortals – or just a
waste of time.

International Association of Assholes
http://thebird.org/assholes

The club with the most eligible number of potential members. Once the association has fleeced a new asshole of their money, said asshole receives a certificate of membership.

Organisation for the Advancement of Facial Hair
www.ragadio.com/oafh

Anyone who pays the slightest attention to the world around them can't have failed to notice the fact that the beard relaunched itself back into mainstream fashion a few years ago via young people's grunge-pop music hailing from Seattle. The sudden popularity of looking like a gibbon must have led to the formation of this group of people. Dealing with all aspects of sporting whiskers, members of this dubious cult are invited to attend meetings with guest beardies. There they can discuss living with a growth and how it psychologically affected them and those around them.

The Potbellied Men of America Club
http://potbelly.com

The Potbellied Men of America Club is the product of that time-honoured story of a man who worships his salt-of-the-earth dad who selfishly dies on him. Being inconsolable, the grieving son decides that the best memorial would be a website encapsulating everything poor old Dad stood for. Who can honestly say that they wouldn't join a club with a motto 'Many Americans live the American Dream; potbellied men DELIVER the American Dream'? Set up to improve the self-esteem of blue-collar potbellied men, the site features a 'Pinup of the Month' with a biog glorifying the hard-working tendencies of this overlooked majority section of US society.

Women Who Pee Standing Up
www.restrooms.org/standing.html

If today's GI Janes can fight as effectively as their male counterparts, they still can't take a leak as easily. The US military pissed away millions of research dollars on this very same problem and came up with the inspired conclusion that they should use a funnel. Could have saved a fortune if they'd bothered to check out this group of resourceful women. Excellent news for today's current crop of geezer birds who can now plumb the levels of the best rugby players around.

Corporations

Having a corporate website is essential for corporate credibility nowadays. What it has shown is that there are some very strange companies out there.

The British Lard Marketing Board   www.blmb.freeserve.co.uk
Fantastic posters of yesteryear will get the public nostalgic for this white artery blocker. There's also a selection of lard-themed music, PC wallpaper and a screensaver.

The Corporation   www.thecorporation.com
Apparently up to twenty pictures of barely legal, clothesless kittens appear every day on the web. The corporation is attempting to protect the world's children by making a minuscule donation of its immense profits to prevent the spread of this kitty porn.

Gap Sucks   www.gapsucks.org
Not everyone's a fan of drab khaki or even the company that is trying to clad the world in it. Particularly, residents of the land in California where the family who own the company are clearing forests at an alarming rate. Join the protest now and rid the world of dreary clothing.

Genetic Savings & Clone   www.savingsandclone.com
Genetic banking for scientists. It's hardly good practice to keep the DNA of endangered species in the back of the fridge. It should be treated with the respect that people's hard-earned savings are, and put into a bank. That's exactly what this is.

Harvey Washbangers www.harveywashbangers.com/firsthwb.html

David Harvey is a man with a keen eye for an unexploited market segment. He realised when he went to college that he would have to do his own laundry and it was a truly unpleasant experience. In an attempt to take the drudgery out of the washday he invented Harvey Washbangers, which combine washing machines with bars, web cafés and dining facilities.

Useless Industries http://uselessindustries.com.

A snapshot into the workings of the world's most pointless multinational. Or is this a vision of twenty-first-century working practices? The advent of a nominal admin fee following a negative performance review may be just around the corner.

19//PLACES TO VISIT

Booking flights online is now cheaper and quicker than a visit to the travel agency. After browsing some travel websites and finding a hotel, you discover that the world suddenly isn't such a big place after all. The web has totally revolutionised the travel industry.

Places to go

A few attractions that probably won't be making it into next year's travel brochures.

The Aparecida Magic, Cultural, Religious and Recreational Park   www.usatoday.com/life/travel/leisure/1999/ltl371.htm
The world's only Catholic theme park, the Vatican excepted. This $70 million Brazilian venture is looking at fleecing pilgrims in the way that other theme parks have been doing for years. The difference is that there's more than tacky souvenirs to leave with.

Atomic Tourist   www.atomictourist.com
If a nice atom tan is more your choice than a sun tan, then this useful little site will make a traditional tour guide superfluous for this year's holiday. Listings include tourist attractions all over the world that have been the site of atomic explosions, display exhibits on the development of atomic devices or contain vehicles that were designed to deliver atomic weapons.

The Bathrooms of Maddison County   www.nutscape.com
A variation on the film of a similar name. While in said place waiting to see said film one couple decided to do a quick road trip of the bridges from the film. After copious cold beverages and even more toilet trips they decided that they'd seen more conveniences than river crossings. So they documented their afternoon's adventures to produce this scat-based road-trip story.

The Best Public Toilets In . . .   www.besttoilets.com
Banish thoughts of the toilet scene from *Trainspotting* when in a foreign city. Never slum it again with this list of the finest latrines for elegant surroundings in your hour of need.

The Budget Traveller's Guide   www3.sympatico.ca/
to Sleeping in Airports   donna.mcsherry/airports.htm
Travellers on a budget don't need to slum it by staying in rat-infested hostels when they know that there's a place with hot running water, shops and restaurants that's open 24 hours a day. Yup, the airport they just landed at is the ultimate free accommodation and this guide offers the best tips for nights of expense-free comfort.

Butts Across
America   http://buttsacrossamerica.com
The web's made mooning universally fashionable again. Instead of the usual 'this is me on holiday with my arse out', users are invited to submit pix of their bottoms enjoying the fresh air at major landmarks and monuments across the USA. The Grand Canyon will never look the same again.

Coney Island   www.coneyislandusa.com/
Circus Sideshow   sideshow.shtml
Certainly not the most politically correct form of entertainment. This blast from the past is still going strong on the fringes of NYC. Current acts on the roster include 'The Fire God', 'Serpentina', 'The Illustrated Man' and 'Koko the Killer Clown'. A definite 'Don't try this at home'.

Crazy Horse   www.crazyhorse.org
Is a tribute to Native Americans rightly peeved that they didn't get a look-in when Mount Rushmore was conceived. A five-hundred-foot face carved into the side of a South Dakota mountain.

Cyber Rodeo　　　　　　　　　　www.cyberrodeo.com

Where the West meets the web. Two Fort Worth cowboy eateries hooked up to the Internet. Truly individual corporate conference venues.

Factual Guide for Americans　　　　　　　www.jomiller.com/
Visiting Britain　　　　　　　　　　　　　　guide

Inflict misery on next year's onslaught of rich, trainer-clad loudmouths. We all apologise for tardiness with the traditional excuse of having had a quick siesta (or 'wank', as it's known in Britain). A delightful afternoon can be spent on the river of one of our university cities: punts are known as yer-I-nals and the means of propulsion is cottaging. Simply ask a policeman the whereabouts of the nearest public yer-I-nals as you wish to partake in a spot of cottaging. The best cuts of beef in a swanky restaurant are those that conform to the British Standard of Excellence commonly known as BSE beef.

Foreigners' Guide　　　　　　　　　www.rotodesign.com/
to America　　　　　　　　　　　　america/america.html

Random generalisations about American culture for people who never crossed the pond.

Haywards Heath　　　　　　　　www.punzel.demon.co.uk

Life in a small town where one of the main attractions is the one-way system and someone thought they saw Stirling Moss drive under the bridge near the station.

Hobbit House　　　　　　　　　www.aloha.net/~hobbit

The ultimate guesthouse for Tolkien fans. Even better – it's in Hawaii.

Llanfairpwllgwyngyllgog-erychwyrndrobwlllla-ntysiliogogogoch http://llanfairpwllgwyngyllgog-erychwyrndrobwlllla-ntysiliogogogoch.co.uk

Not only the village with the longest name in Britain but the longest URL on the web. Nobody's going to be able to type this in properly. Just go to Ask Jeeves (**www.ask.com**) and ask for the longest URL.

Mississippi Trailer Park www.drbukk.com/gmhom/park.html

Those unfortunate enough to end up living in an American trailer park come in for a lot of flack from patronising house dwellers. Take a tour of some of the more unusual customised mobile homes in Mississippi, where standing out means an accompanying car on bricks and a homicidal pit bull.

Motels for Train Watchers http://home.att.net/~roadrailer/MotelsIntro.html

Excellent! No longer are normal hotel residents in danger of bumping into beige-wearing, halitosis-afflicted men with notebooks when they're trying to whoop it up in the bar. Surely, compiling a list of hotels for trainspotters is a form of supertrainspotting?

Outhouses of America www.jldr.com/ohindex.shtml

Obviously symptomatic of a compulsive obsession with these fresh-air inconveniences and should be treated with a quick course of therapy.

Roadside America www.roadsideamerica.com

Guide to offbeat tourism in the States. Living proof that the sweeping globalisation of multinational corporations will never break the spirits of life's true individuals.

Sign the Mars Petition http://space.thinkmars.net/petition/addpetition.html

Space cadets, use your collective might to persuade the US president that the world wants to do a bit of space tourism. The target is over a million email addresses by the time the new president is sworn in.

Soup & Sandwich   www.oscar-mayer.com/soup.n.sandwich/placenamemap.html

Ridiculous places in America that have a food-based name. Ever fancied visiting Bread Tray Mountain in Texas or Tomato Can Creek in Montana? Thought not.

Surreal Southend   www.surreal-southend.co.uk

Could there be more to Southend-on-Sea than meets the eye? Probably not, but the author of this site is dedicated 'to collecting evidence of unusual activity by people in the past and present'. His best exhibit in his defence is a giant cat lurking in the library. Watch out for the men in white coats.

The Tackiest Place in America Contest   www.thepoint.net/~usul/text/tacky.html

No shortage of entries for this competition. The fifty-foot Indian, Carhenge, the Roadkill Café and a building shaped like a bulldozer look pretty unbeatable, but there are sure to be plenty of surprises left.

Tour De Butt   www.tourdebutt.com

Bare-arsed cheek and travelling. One man's quest to travel to exotic places and reveal his butt for the camera. Bet he never visits a Muslim country, though.

Urinal net   www.urinal.net

Apparently the best place to piss away your time on the Internet. Never be caught short again with this global guide to the best watering holes.

White Trash Café   www.whitetrashcafe.com

The Hard Rock Café, Planet Hollywood, Fashion Café, Motown Café and Harley Davidson Café – tacky tourist traps. Is the day of the theme café over? Apparently not.

Ways to get there

It's not the destination, it's the journey, as so many people have said throughout the ages.

Airport City Codes   www.airportcitycodes.com

Plane spotter Mecca, including codes for 9,000 airports worldwide and runway length, elevation, latitude and longitude. More amusing are the top-ten lists of how people behave on planes and whimsical stories about in-flight behaviour.

Airtoons   www.airtoons.com

Those airline safety cards are just so boring that nobody's ever going to pay any attention to them. With the aid of startling captions, common-or-garden flying scenes are given a whole surreal lease of life. If these ones were ever slipped into a plane there would be no need for any more in-flight entertainment.

The Bus Plunge   www.busplunge.org

Picture this – package holiday of a lifetime, hotel still an hour away, tortuous mountain roads, breakneck speeds, fourteen-year-old bus driver (possibly drunk), visions of *The Italian Job*, suffering the ignominy of a tiresome relative calming all around with utterances to the effect that '. . . they do this every day. They're fantastic drivers . . .' Well they're not. As the Bus Plunge so graphically illustrates.

Military Vehicle Broker &   http://brightnet.
Appraisal Service   horizontel.com/mvs

Interesting trades considered, apparently. Fancy upgrading the people carrier for something with a bit more city attitude? This is the place where the only way to do the school run is in an armoured personnel carrier.

No Shitting in   www.magna.com.au/
the Toilet   ~nglobe/nsitt/topic.html

The privileged business traveller apart, air travel is just about the most uncomfortable form of public transport ever devised. This site has collated some of the most annoying aspects, such as pallid airline food, airport taxi drivers and the most monstrous of all – the middle-aged, frumpy air hostess who seems to have real problems with backpackers and their natural urge to drink as much free booze and eat as many complimentary peanuts as possible.

Rabbi Goodvench's   www.morecrap.com/
Car Care Tips   carcare.htm

Forget Jeremy Clarkson – when it comes to good old-fashioned auto maintenance Rabbi Goodvench's Car Care Tips are what any budding Michael Shumacher needs. How do I stop my speedo cable howling? Check it's not a pregnant woman. I didn't notice I'd hit her till she went into labour and she started screaming . . .

Rent-A-Wreck   http://rent-a-wreck.com

Jalopy rental business. When the bland hire car just won't do.

The Rollerpup 900   www.ecrap.com

An electric skate-tow vehicle for lazy rollerbladers. A bit like a motorised Zimmer frame – which is probably what its owners will need after being dragged into oncoming traffic by one of these ridiculous devices.

The Skycar   www.moller.com/skycar

Moller International has developed the first and only feasible, personally affordable, personal vertical-takeoff-and-landing (VTOL) vehicle the world has ever seen. Steal the thunder of every flash git in the world by turning up to the pub in this little beauty.

Speedtrap Registry   **www.speedtrap.com**

The Holy Grail of driving: motor like a demon and retain your licence. Well, that's the theory. More likely crash into a tree while trying to read your printouts.

Tube Hell   **www.tubehell.com**

London dwellers who've encountered just one jabbering tramp or fetid armpit too many on their daily commute can vent a bit of steam here.

Ugliest Cars in Britain   **www.uglycars.co.uk**

British car designers don't seem to have been blessed with the same kind of design talent as their Italian counterparts. This site brings you the most hideous vehicles ever to disgrace the nation's highways. Even better are the ugliness ratings in the form of 'the number of paper bags you'd have to put on your head before accepting a lift'.

20//POLITICS

With the web, everyone's got a soapbox. There's a deafening melée of wackos out there just dying to get their point across.

Are You a Terrorist?   **www.new-labour.com**
Recent changes in the anti-terrorist laws in the UK mean that even the slightest subversive thought could bring you a visit from the Home Office. Even *thinking* that Nelson Mandela is a groovy old guy with a nice wardrobe of shirts could have the storm troopers banging down your front door. This parodic website is actually trying to get across a serious message and, after you've taken the New Labour Terrorist Lottery scratch-card test and the 'Am I a Terrorist?' interactive quiz, you may find it best to keep your mouth shut in future.

Jello Biafra For President   **www.angelfire.com/punk/jello2000**
Punk-rock Presidential hopeful Jello Biafra, the screaming frontman of the Dead Kennedys, has decided to stop bitching about the corporate world and take it on. He's standing on a Green Party ticket. After years of spoken-word ranting about conspiracy theories, he's going to become one of his own.

The Seed   **www.soi.city.ac.uk/~louise/seed2.html**
This is exactly what the web is good for: expressing underground opinion and news. The Seed is a British site about freedom and anarchy. Although how they ever come to a consensus about what they publish is anyone's guess.

Skeleton Closet   **www.realchange.org**
Politicians seem to lurch from one scandal to another and have a disarming habit of shaking off any lingering tarnish. This is one site that isn't going to let them forget their tawdry pasts. Lots of scurrilous dirt on all US presidential candidates, just to remind people with short memories what they're really voting for.

Smurf Communism   www.users.zetnet.co.uk/govinda/smurfs

If rampant political correctness was the scourge of the mid-80s mindset, its roots can be directly traced back to the loose thinking and morals of mid-70s TV programme commissioners and their ilk. Particularly the team responsible for the conception of Father Abraham and his 'family'. Finally, the little blue critters have been nailed as the subversive mindbenders that they really were. This site presents the evidence. Senator McCarthy probably would've missed the similarities between Karl Marx and Papa Smurf or Brainy Smurf and Trotsky, but it's all here.

Who Wants to Be   www.phoenixnewtimes.com/
a President?   extra/president/game.html

Good point. Being the most powerful man in the world does have its drawbacks. Like not being able to take a leak without the secret service monitoring it. This game tests whether you'd cut the presidential mustard by asking a series of tricky questions and rating the number of votes you'd get.

Gender politics

While most of these sites are not about the front line of the struggle of the sexes, they contain all the best 'post-modern stuff squarely aimed at females' ezines out there. Hilarious, attitude by the bucketload and taking no crap from the men in the world.

Chick Click   www.chickclick.com

A power network for independent women's sites with a claimed readership of over a million people. Total lifestyle coverage.

Gurl.com   www.gurl.com

Anarchic-looking ezine with lots of advice, skateboarding, e-postcards, message boards and free email.

Heartless Bitch   www.heartless-bitches.com

Anyone with the limited psychic ability of Mystic Meg can see that the Spices' brand of Girl Power is likely to have the longevity of the average torch battery. The real McCoy delivers in the form of *Heartless Bitch*, which is the all-encompassing lifestyle guide for snotty chicks that leaves the most testosteroned-up MCP quivering in his Calvin's. 'Sappy Site of the Day' (for non-lovers everywhere) could put Interflora out of business; 'They Shouldn't Be Allowed To Breed' could elicit a few court cases; and 'Deal With It' (coping with the inconsistencies of post-fem culture) is tubthumbing par excellence. Dangerous stuff.

Riot Grrl   www.riotgrrl.com

Oozing attitude – men, beware! Highlights include supermodel wrestling, feeding a supermodel, 'Riotgrrl', an oracle and 'Sexriot', which explores the sexuality of some of today's more ambiguous superstars.

Smile and Act Nice   www.smileandactnice.com

Predictably pink and claiming 'In girls we trust'. Featuring relationship advice from the Ho in the Know.

The Werewolf's   http://
Armpits   werewolfs.armpits.homepage.com

Dispelling the myth that feminists are a bunch of humourless women with hairy armpits is *The Werewolf's Armpits*, proving that it's possible to cultivate underarm flora and still raise a giggle. Sections such as 'Why All Women Should Have Hairy Armpits' and the 'Right Wing Oscars', it's a right-on feminist ezine that may just scare the willies off any faint-hearted man who dares to enter.

21//REAL PEOPLE

Most people practise their HTML skills on the very mundane websites that generally feature themselves. These sites usually involve pictures of the owner and an excruciating list of their favourite hobbies and weblinks. They can't be under the illusion that anyone's actually interested, but they're a good start before they become web celebrities.

Aaron & Carmen   www.geocities.com/carmen_n_aaron
'I wanted to buy you something special for Valentine's day but decided to make you something that you could treasure for ever' are the opening words of this online atrocity. Roughly translated as 'I'm too lazy and mean to buy you a decent present but I can scan in a few photos and garnish them with some amorous hyperbole.' Get down the shops next year.

The Amazing World of Brad Byers   www.bradbyers.com
A world-class professional loony who does things that most people couldn't bear to watch. He holds the world record for swallowing eight 28-inch swords and hammering tools into his nostrils, so he's not a man to mess with. Other delights in his repertoire include putting tarantulas and scorpions in his mouth, lying on beds of nails and the less perilous yo-yo act. Book him online for weddings, bar mitzvahs and christenings.

Amy's Answering Machine   www.sendamy.com
Amy Borkowsky has a problem: her mother just won't stop phoning her. Even her first line of defence, her answering machine, isn't enough to keep the persistent matriarch at bay. Being the enterprising soul she is, Amy kept all the answerphone messages and put them up on her own website. So successful was the endeavour she's managed to make a CD of the calls. Find out what it's like to be stalked by a member of your own family here.

Big Mike World   **www.keywestparadise.com/**
Largest Bartender   **bigmike.html**
Barefoot Bob's Bar & Restaurant in Key West boasts the world's
largest barman and probably the smallest number of brawls. Here is
Big Mike in all his gargantuan glory.

Burslem's Witch   **www.geocities.com/potteries_2000**
An insight into the boredom and paranoia of England in the Middle
Ages. Molly Leigh was born in 1685 in Burslem, Staffordshire, and,
by virtue of the fact that she was born an 'ugly' child who skipped
church and made friends with a blackbird, her fellow villagers
thought she was a witch. There are plenty of TV celebrities today
guilty of exactly the same things, so maybe they weren't all wrong.
When she died her natural death the local clergy still wouldn't let
her be, and dug her up and turned the body over to give her a bit of
peace.

Dale's Skirt Pages   **www.aristotle.net/~domiller/gallery.html**
Dale Miller is a pretty ordinary, middle-aged guy with a pretty good
job and life. What sets him apart from his fellow male-menopause
victims is his penchant for skirt wearing. Not in a flashy Danny la
Rue kind of way, but in exactly the same way his female
counterparts would. The pictures make for startling viewing when it
becomes apparent that Dale is built like an outdoor commode – but
highly amusing none the less.

Dead Mike   **www.deadmike.com/indexNS.html**
Luckily he's not, but he nearly was. After being suckered into a
charity parachute jump, the nearly Dead Mike found himself
free-falling with no chance of his chutes opening. Fortune prevailed
and he survived with a medley of injuries that would make Evel
Kneivel's eyes pop. During his prolonged convalescence he armed
himself with a laptop and set about this marvellous tirade against
the dangers of skydiving. Never set foot in a plane again.

Disneyland Fashion   http://pattywack.com/tpfashions.html

It's a horrible thing to say but the kind of people who yearn to visit Disneyland aren't going to be the most high-class travellers. There's just a huge possibility that they're not going to be the most elegantly dressed, either. Just what fashion atrocities they inflict on their fellow tourists is here for all the world to see.

Dot Com guy   www.dotcomguy.com

Before he took on his current alter ego the Dot Com guy was a normal nine-to-fiver. Shortly after moving to his new pad, he spent an afternoon being dragged around several local department stores by his parents. Moaning throughout the incident, he claimed that he could have bought all his stuff over the web far less painfully. In fact it would be even better if he could get it all from his PC and not pay for it, so he decided to try to live off the web for a year. Find out how he's getting on via webcasts and video cameras through his website.

Fugly   www.fugly.net

The point of most individuals' homepages is, to be honest, just an excuse to practise their coding skills in case they ever have an idea worthy of a decent website. The number of pointless 'I'm XXX – here's my homepage . . .' sites is enormous. One talented individual has realised that there are a lot of pictures of very ordinary and sometimes ugly people posted up on these tedious sites, so he decided to find them, steal them and put them up on his own website for people to laugh at.

The Guillotine Fressie's   www.algonet.se/~giljotin/
Home Page   fressie.html

The vociferous Guillotine Fressie is probably the only instrument of mass execution to have its own website. Not *dedicated* to it, exactly, but just like everyone else, it wants to tell the world about their mundane existence on free webpages. It currently resides in the Swedish home of its owner and part-time dominatrix Mrs

Berliner-Mauer, and it's a bit of a shock to find out that guillotines have feelings too.

The Hairy Human's Homepage www.luna.co.uk/~charles
Hairy Human is a hirsute forty-year-old Surrey taxi driver who looks like a cross between a gibbon and a werewolf. He reckons he's got a serious medical condition and you can share his predicament through these web pages.

How Fresh is This Guy? www.howfreshisthisguy.com
Another collection of real-people websites. How fresh are they? Not very. They're all a bit cheesy and creepy. A gruesome collection of all that is bad in American men.

Interactive Underwear www.moosenet.com/iu.html
Frieda and Guido are a normal-looking Californian couple whose solution to spicing up their flagging sex life involves inviting people to send them underwear. Not only do they wear the clothes, but they also take pictures of themselves and post them on this website like the good exhibitionists they are. So any donors are treated to pictures of a scantily clad middle-aged couple parading their gift. At least they're appreciative.

I Wanna Be Famous www.iwannabefamous.com
The origins of this site can almost certainly be traced to that dreadful Bros song. Like a virtual talent contest, iwannabefamous.com features ordinary people with a taste for exhibitionism doing extraordinary things. The chances are slim that anyone other than the friends and relatives of the participants have the slightest interest in what these highly unique individuals have to offer, but a daily procession of 'Everyone look at me, I'm great' type people grace the pages.

Jim & Tim the Duct Tape Guys www.ducttapeguys.com
It started off as a drunken college prank when a couple of students had enough time on their hands to stage a duct-tape crucifixion to

become the Duct Tape Jesus. From that point onwards Jim and Tim became the duct-tape guys and set out to tell the world all the 'other' uses for this remarkable DIY material, which has spun out into lucrative book deals and comedy acts. Sticky tape will never be the same again.

Joe & Natalie's Naked page
http://home.onestop.net/ nakednatalie.com/naked.html

How unusual for a couple of naturists to be exhibitionists! Joe and Natalie are not content with showing off with clothes-free supermarket shopping or bouncing balls at table tennis and volleyball like other advocates of the clothes-free lifestyle. Instead they take their showing off to global proportions by evangelising through their own website. To show how completely well adjusted they are they've even taken this opportunity to advertise their businesses. Anyone need some nudey graphic design done? This is the place.

Lady Lynn's Huggs
www.angelfire.com/ma/ladylynn

Lady Lynn sounds like one of those sixties drug casualties who continue to preach love and peace to the world. On her web pages she delivers a selection of supposedly heartfelt 'hugs' to various family members and loved ones. The whole thing in its pink/ lavender hues is an assault on the eyeballs, and in all about as sickening as sticking your fingers down your throat.

LA's Most Wanted Delinquent Parents
http://da.co.la.ca.us/ childsupport/delinquent15.htm

Most highly sensitive, hormonally wired teenagers are acutely embarrassed by the actions of their parents. In fact it's not unheard of for members of the complexion-challenged generation to disown them for the slightest misdemeanour. This site will convince them that the whole world is against them as the LA authorities have conspired to show the world that this group of parents are a bunch of inadequate losers.

Marine Corps Wives   www.marinewives.com

What happens to the spouses of America's war heroes when they're off fighting the enemies of Uncle Sam? You've got it: nobody knows – or didn't until BJ Chadduck, a lovesick ex-marine, set up a site specifically for his wife and the thousands of others like her. The result is a virtual community for wives who are wondering what their absent husbands are up to. As he keeps saying, he did it all because he loves his wife, or bought a new PC. Or something.

Mr Methane   www.mrmethane.com

The 'world's only performing flatulist', who bears an uncanny resemblance to the Mr Muscle character from the TV ads. Truly an anal virtuoso, Mr Methane actually earns a living from performing his fart act to incredulous audiences around the globe. Book him for the next Masonic Lodge meeting.

My Boot   www.myboot.com

The interminable life of Craig Mitchell and his novella about a relationship with a girlfriend, the endearingly titled, *She Hates My Futon*. He also writes about his favourite search engines sending him up the wrong path. A great example of a man who needs a more fulfilling job.

Online Memorial   www.tir.com/~frank04

Scott Amedure was the first very real victim of America's talk-show culture. When his best friend, Jon Schmitz, was invited to appear on *The Jenny Jones Show*, he didn't realise that his secret admirer was Scott. To say he was not impressed is an understatement. Unable to cope with the public embarrassment, he stalked his ex-buddy and murdered him. This is his fascinating memorial, which gives details of the ensuing court cases.

Rubberburner   www.rubberburner.com

Another 'I'm dying for a shag, please get in touch' site. Curry (his name apparently) is an unreconstructed guy who likes racing cars and growing long, poodle-style, heavy-metal hair. And he's looking for ladies. Any girls with a thing for redneck grease monkeys should head his way.

The Society to Prevent   **http://egomania.nu/**
My Employment   **causes/indexsoc.html**

Now everyone's at it. Stories abound of people trying to dodge work by listing gifts they've received on their websites. Princess Natalie thinks she's far too precocious and talented to have to work for a living like normal people – and who are we to disagree? Anyone who agrees enough to send her money to support her less than unique lifestyle choice can send it via the address above.

Strictly Private   **www.lordbath.co.uk**

That bonkers posh bloke the Marquis of Bath shares his thoughts with the plebs. Find out all about his paintings, writings, ideas on life, poetry and songs, photographs of the family and friends, and other detail that throws light on his eccentric lifestyle. This is, after all, a man who keeps lions in his garden, so he should have something fairly interesting to say.

10k4awife.com   **www.10k4awife.com**

Rod Barnett is either most people's idea of a sad net nerd with too much money and inadequate social skills, or a modern realist. One day he woke up and realised that his life was marching on, he had no one to share his money with and his lifestyle was offering no prospects of meeting his perfect partner. He decided to forgo dating agencies and offer ten thousand dollars to anyone who introduced him to his future wife. Presumably, after being offered numerous scamsters, he's actually met someone who takes his fancy because the good news is that he's currently dating.

Things My Girlfriend And I   **www.wlv.ac.uk/**
Have Argued About   **~in5185**

As if it were not bad enough enduring couples fighting in public, this site is a form of virtual eavesdropping. A record of one real life couple's relationship ups and downs mapped out in excruciating detail. It's an education scrolling down the argument's topic list, which extends even to the best way to cut kiwi fruit and what's the best seat in the cinema. It's good to see that it's not only your other half who can be unreasonable.

Ugly People   www.uglypeople.com
Online circus side show. Laugh at the unfortunate freaks.

Winston   www.geocities.com/
Homepage   SiliconValley/Sector/8560
Computer programmers don't do themselves any favours when it comes to dispelling the image that they're social inadequates, likely to go postal at the merest hint of rejection from people they've gone sweet on. A quick glimpse at the Winston homepage will leave people wondering whether only a spoof site could be this bad. The hero preaches that we should 'eat right and exercise'. Unfortunately his exercise is wrestling and massage, as his obviously authentic letters of recommendation from lovely ladeez will testify.

The World's Strongest Morons   http://moron.strongestman.com
Place two or three jocks within the close vicinity of beer, and testosterone levels inevitably rise and the showing off begins. Few people will marvel at these feats of inebriated machismo, but visitors will leave with a smug air of intellectual superiority.

22//RELIGION

Eternal damnation awaits the authors of most of these spoof religious sites. With the Internet being used as the weapon of choice at the front line of religious evangelism, it was only a matter of time before a bunch of Smart Alecs decided to poke a little fun.

Ask Sister Rosetta   www.rossetta.com
She fearlessly confronts such thorny issues as sleeping in the nude – what would Jesus do? She also outlines Bible-approved vs. unauthorised underwear.

Bastard Son of the Lord   www.bsotl.org
The darker side of Christianity. Ask Jesus for some advice and check out all the (genuine) hate mail.

Bible Story Madlibs   www.mcs.net/~pookie/madlibs.html
For the more religious web-head, Bible Story Madlibs religious satire goes online. The Greatest Story Ever Told reaches new heights of absurdity because it can be tailored to the needs of the modern netizen. There's no need to suffer the embarrassment of trying to pronounce tongue-twisting names such as Thessalonians when 'Kevin's mates' will suffice. The loaves-and-fishes story can be brought bang up to date by scripting it in an a supermarket car park and dishing out chicken Kievs and garlic bread. On the negative side, eternal damnation is assured with an omnipresent deity lurking in your computer's hard drive.

The Christian's Guide   www.frii.com/~gosplow/
to Small Arms   cgsa.html
Christians have for centuries been twisting passages from the Bible into some of the most fantastic excuses to do whatever they want. A particularly liberal interpretation has given divine authority to this bunch of gun-totin' hicks.

Church of SubGenius   **www.subgenius.com**
This was one of the Internet's first comedy churches. Headed by the mystical smoking head of Bob Dobbs, it's a bonkers amalgam of anarchic humour.

Church of the Virus   **www.lucifer.com/virus**
A pseudo-intellectual experience that celebrates the concept of memes – Collections of mutually supporting ideas. Lots of ideological muscle flexing and very little substance.

Curse Free   **www.cursefree.com**
For boring parents everywhere comes this device for removing cursing from TV and videos. In two years, apparently, TV swearing rose by a third to nearly ninety words per hour. So it's possible to blame the school with certainty when they come back swearing like troopers.

Devil Worship.com   **www.devilworship.com**
Nothing here but a domain for sale. Get it while it's hot and show the world how much you like sacrificing virgins and burning down churches.

Extreme Teen Bible   **www.nelsonbibles.com/extreme**
In an attempt to make the Bible a little more palatable to the current generation of crack-smoking skateboarders, it's got a little more street. Any time soon expect 'Snowboarding for Jesus' and 'God's a Real Gnarly Dude'.

The First Presleyterian Church   chelsea.ios.com/%7Ehkarlin1/
of Elvis the Divine   welcome1.html
Join the church where all male members are required to overindulge in worldly pleasures. They must overeat fatty foods and lead debauched lives of gaudy excess, while their wives must do the housework in bikinis.

The God http://jraxis.kracked.com/
Simulator atheism/simulator/main.html

Have you ever wondered what it would be like to be God? Here's your chance to find out. Spend a few wistful minutes pondering the problems of omnipotence.

The Gospel According www.atl.mindspring.com/
To Lego ~lewval3/pages/gospel.htm

Biblical scriptures elucidated through sticky plastic bricks.

Have Your Baptism http://infoweb.magi.com/
Removed ~godfree/debap.html

The Humanist Association of Canada will 'sever your ties to religion completely' and 'block the effects of any future superstitious rites'. After all, when you're a few weeks old you don't exactly get a choice in your religious send-off. One satisfied customer claims, 'Since having my baptism removed my mind is more clear, the mornings seem brighter and food tastes sooo much better! Now, if I could only find a virginity restoration service I'd be all set for the second half of my life.'

Hell.com www.hell.com

After asking 'Where do you want to go?' it directs you to no-such.com, where you get to choose your fate. Both options go to the same place, which has a sign saying 'GOING DOWN', which closes the browser as soon as you click on it.

Holy Grail: Chalice http://home.fireplug.net/~rshand/
or Manna Machine? streams/science/chalice.html

How can a simple chalice provide food for the followers of Jesus? The significance of this oft-sought religious artefact is nothing to do with its holy connotations but for its possible use in ending world hunger. The evidence is all here.

The Homepage
of Jesus

http://members.aol.com/
Jesus316/index.htm

If everyone else can have their own homepage then why can't the
Son of God?

Jesus Christ on
a Pogostick

www.enteract.com/~guru/
java/pogo.html

After Christ on a bike, here he comes bouncing down the road.
Includes pictures and a screensaver.

Jesus Christ's
Answerphone

http://members.tripod.com/
~jesus_christ

The death knells of organised Christianity can be clearly heard,
courtesy of new media. If this particular supreme deity is indeed
omnipresent then who can explain the existence of such a device?

Jesus of the Week

www.jesusoftheweek.com

Using state-of-the-art Jesitronics, this organisation is redressing any
brand-image shortcomings in the Jesus department. They reckon
that after 2,000 years it's time the guy got a makeover. Well, they're
trying to get people to send their drawings in to win a $2,000 prize
from the *National Catholic Reporter* magazine. Whether anyone
will ever see their money if the design wins is anyone's guess.

Jesus Was a Vegetarian

www.jesusveg.com

There they go again. Reading the scriptures at a special angle in a
certain type of light to prove that Jesus was a veggie. If he'd had his
way it would have been tofu and organic bread for everyone that
day on the mount. Curiously absent are the reasons for his
collaboration with the Piscean oppressors.

Know Your
Patron Saint

www.magna.com.au/
~raymond/patrnsaints.htm

There seems to be a saint for every occasion: driving, brushing your
teeth, bungee jumping. This is the definitive list of what the 2,000
recognised saints get up to.

Last Rites   http://darkimages.com

Nothing says you're a people person like a satanic tattoo, and unfortunately Last Rites is no joke: a genuine devil-worshipping skin-inker. In addition to diabolic skin art (including a full-back study of John the Baptist's head on a platter) discover ten reasons to 'Have a Beer Rather Than a God' before selling your soul to Old Nick just to get on their mailing list.

National Rifle Association   http://choir.faithweb.com/
Christian Bible Choir   info.html

Screaming rednecks with bibles and guns, a scary thought. Anyone who happens to want to combine these two activities and to meet like-minded individuals should look no further than here. The rest of us can run like the wind.

The Pagan Federation   www.paganfed.demon.co.uk

A group working for the religious rights of pagans. So if you fancy dancing around the woods naked, sacrificing the odd virgin or turning people into frogs then this site will tell you how. Well, maybe not, but anyone who fancies a wedding with a difference – or a truly spectacular Hallowe'en – would be well advised to take a peek.

PinStruck   www.pinstruck.com

Just the thing if you can't free up some time to get down to your local voodoo store. If you're burning to get revenge on an enemy then do it online by sending them personalised voodoo curses via email.

Ship of Fools   http://ship-of-fools.com

The magazine of Christian unrest. Find out what the Pope's up to and inspect an exciting range of gadgets for God, including the 'Return to sender' coffin and a metre-high praying-hands sculpture.

The Skeptic's Annotated Bible www.skepticsannotatedbible.com

Nobody would deny that the Bible is full of contradictions and stuffed with gobbledegook padding. The religious establishment has traditionally glossed over this and concentrated on the familiar, but now there's a version of the King James Bible that highlights the nonsense just to embarrass the people who live by the word of the Lord.

The Spectacular Millennium Cross! www.neontrim.com/cross.html

A particularly classy present for a religious aunt. Apparently this is a luminescent masterpiece that combines a religious article with year 2000 technology. Well, it's battery-powered, to drag this fully illuminated religious icon down to Blackpool souvenir levels.

The Temple of the Workshy www.geocities.com/Athens/Parthenon/1514

Web browsing has fast become the activity of choice for the lazy employee. This is their Mecca with an endless supply of amusing stories and excuses for not knuckling down.

Ten Commandments for Handbell Ringers www.jjonline.com/ringing/10commandments.asp

Just because they hang out in churches, it doesn't mean they're above the law of the Almighty. Eternal damnation awaits those who steal their neighbour's pencils or tap their feet with excessive loudness.

The Toast Bible www.vex.net/~smarry/yip/toastbib.html

On the first day he created light, but when did he invent toast? This is the place to read a recently discovered alternative version of the Bible in which toast takes its rightful place in the order of things. We eagerly await Marmite Psalms.

24 Hour Church of Elvis   www.churchofelvis.com

When being a fan becomes a religion. Inevitably the icon of the twentieth century should spawn his own round-the-clock church.

Universal Life Church   **www.ulc.org**

The Universal Life Church will ordain anyone who asks without question of faith, for life, without a fee. The church has two tenets: to guarantee the freedom of religion and to do what is right. A genuine American church set up as a tax scam where you can become an ordained minister for free and work your way up to bishop for a small donation.

**The Virtual Church of
the Blind Chihuahua**   **www.dogchurch.org**

You can't go wrong joining a church whose motto is 'the courage to be ridiculous before God'. It's a truly sacred place in cyberspace named in honour of a little old dog with cataracts, which barked sideways at strangers because he couldn't see where they were. Apparently, humans relate to God in the same way, making a more or less joyful noise in God's general direction, and expecting a reward for doing so. Join a tour around the church and take a Sunday school lesson with a difference – the ethics of high school sex. True believers can even dip into the Book of Uncommon Worship and receive Benediction for Middle Managers Before Annual Performance Appraisals and discover 'the best and most useful lie' . . .

Voodoo Assassination Project   **www.javigate.com/TVAP**

Attempts to identify the world's most hated celebrities and then assist their untimely demise through the torture of small plastic effigies. Just don't get too close to the Spice Girls.

Voodoo Cultural   **www.folkart.com/
Centre & Collection**   **~latitude/voodooshop/**

Visitors to New Orleans need never be caught short in the voodoo department. Drop in for all ritualistic accessories and buy online from home. Just don't ask for Barbie.

23//SCIENCE & TECHNOLOGY

The perfect medium of communication for technically minded people, the Internet has long been the nerd's preferred form of swapping ideas. It's also become the way that wackos with a gift want to preach their unique messages.

Science

A long time ago the web was used as a method for scientists to communicate and further the quest for knowledge. It's not like that any more. Well, maybe a little bit, but the web is full of mad amateur scientists desperately searching for recognition.

Bunny Survival Tests　　　　**www.pcola.gulf.net/~irving/bunnies**
If there were an alternative Nobel Prize, then this scientific endeavour would be a prime contender. Put simply, two bored scientists set out to determine specific weaknesses and/or strengths possessed by 'Marshmallow Bunnies'. It includes laser exposure endurance, flame, electrocution and radiation tolerance. Best of all is the coyote test, which involves tying the victims to a brick and dropping them out of a window.

The Cat Scan Contest　　　　**www.cat-scan.com**
The CAT scan was a significant contribution to medical science; the Cat Scan Contest is a significant contribution to animal cruelty. Simply flatten your moggy on to a computer scanner and send in the results.

Chapter II –
The Bunnies Strike Back　　　　**http://marks.networktel.net**
A web sequel to the Bunny Survival tests which includes dying in the rain, BOOM!, and the deep freeze.

Experiments With Which You Shall Ruin Stuff and Learn Science at the Same Time
www.geocities.com/SunsetStrip/Palms/6288/exp.html

Making science genuinely exciting. It includes the canned-food experiment, which involves exploding canned food, and the scissor-jack experiment, which involves loosening a rock face to cause a minor avalanche and destroy a car parked at the bottom of a hill.

Head Explosion
www.smart.net/~kenny/explode.htm

A terrifying new condition that culminates in people's heads exploding, as first suffered by a Russian chess champion. Check out the warning symptoms, such as 'thinking too hard', and switch on the TV and crack a tin of beer.

Hypothetical Planets
http://203.230.169.10/solar/hypothet.htm

There have been a number of objects that were once thought by astronomers to exist, but later 'vanished'. These are their stories.

Infectious Cases of the Month
www.pds.med.umich.edu/users/greenson/infectcasesmonth.htm

Like a Page 3 for microbiologists. Every month the University of Michigan chooses an infectious disease for our delectation. So, if *Helicobacter pylori* is your thing, then this is your place.

Mad Science
www.rdsltd.demon.co.uk

Or, more accurately, drunk science. A group of individuals whose goal is to solve all the mysteries of science, through outrageous speculation and excessive abuse of alcohol. Not sure why they think they're so different from the rest of the science community.

MAD Scientist Network
www.madsci.org

The laboratory that never sleeps. Initially set up as a Washington University Young Scientist programme to improve science literacy, it's now a global network of scientists all primed to answer your questions. So, if you've ever been baffled by science, this is the place to ask.

Mars Society **www.marssociety.org.uk**

A collective of people dedicated to setting foot on Mars at some point. Their mission is to lobby governments until they give in and spend all their money on space-travel research. A big hit with Trekkies, no doubt.

Metal Storm **www.scientificamerican.com/1999/0499issue/0499techbus2.html**

This is an electronic gun with no mechanical parts that fires a million rounds per minute – and that's *got* to be enough for even the most hardcore drive-by aficionado. It was invented by a lone Australian tinkerer, which is quite lucky, because if he had any neighbours they'd have had nervous breakdowns by now.

Online Pregnancy Test **www.fosml.com/pregnant**

A must for the compulsive bed-hopper who can't be bothered to leave the office or is too cheap or embarrassed to go to the pharmacy. This free service claims to work regardless of gender.

Patently Absurd **www.patent.freeserve.co.uk**

Being able to prove that an invention belongs to you is an essential part of corporate research. The ideas are generally unintelligible to the outside world, but it's the tin-pot inventors who apply for patents who make the people laugh. This is a collection of genuine inventions that have been patented. Including nonspinning golf balls with flaps and a device to stop long-eared dogs getting dirty when eating.

Pink, the Flavour **www.jonessoda.com/files/pink.html**

The crazy guys at Jones Soda have decided that pink is a flavour for their beverages. Their patent for the flavour blue is presumably not so far away.

Psycho History **www.psychohistory.com**

Not a history of serial killers but an analysis of how leaders' personalities have affected their leadership. Human history is apparently shaped by human emotional traumas – for example, Reagan's castration complex. And the Gulf War was George Bush's revenge on an angry dad.

Restrooms of the Future   **www.restrooms.org**
A genuine site dedicated to speculation as to the contents of our future toilets. Totally lacking in interest until a scroll down the page reveals an item on how women can pee standing up.

Search for Extraterrestrial   **http://setiathome.**
Intelligence   **ssl.berkeley.edu**
SETI@home is a scientific experiment that uses Internet-connected computers in the search for little green men. Download a mesmerising screensaver that shows how your PC is analysing scraps of data from radio telescopes.

Strange Science   **www.turnpike.net/~mscott**
Science is a bit of a hit-and-miss affair. The great advances tend to obscure the crackpot notions and hare-brained theories that get swept under the carpet before bringing the discipline into disrepute. Things that we now take for granted, like dinosaurs, were once the subject of intense and furious debate. This site chronicles some of the misguided postulations that tried to explain what we take for granted today.

Typing Injury FAQ   **www.tifaq.org**
PCs may be great as communication devices but getting data into them still uses technology that's hundreds of years old. When Internet addiction leads to talk about repetitive-strain injuries, this is the place to find a cure.

Virtual Autopsy   **www.le.ac.uk/pathology/teach/va2**
For the budding Quincy who can't muster up the courage for a little Burke-and-Hare grave robbing, Leicester University have devised their own PC post-mortem.

The Wacky Patent of the Month http://colitz.com/site/wacky.htm
Not so much a compendium of mad patents, more of a breaking-
news service for more imaginative inventors.

___

Technology

___

*The best way for technophiles to indulge their obsession. These
websites may not be the best use of technology but they're all based
on an interesting idea.*

Actual Calls and Letters www.shadowstorm.com/
to Internet Technical Support tech_support
One tech support worker tells the stories of his two years of hell at
the hands of the world's most inept customers. You'll never be
stroppy when asking for help again.

Bugblaster High-Powered www.repairfaq.org/sam/
Laser laserpic/bbsrpics.htm#bbsrtoc
Right on, get those little critters. Build this masterpiece and fly spray
will be a thing of the past as you get to play *Star Wars* in your own
house.

The Dead Media Project www.wps.com/dead-media
Takes the cyberpunk godfather Bruce Sterling's *Dead Media
Manifesto* to extremes. This is a graveyard for technologies that
have fallen out of favour.

Fun with Surges www.netcomuk.co.uk/~wwl/surge.html
A surge generator provides short spikes of electricity. The owner of
this site bought one at an auction and decided to see how many
things he could destroy with it.

Hacker News www.hackernews.com
Brian Martin is watching them watching us. All the latest gossip on
net terrorists. Just be careful not to upset them or you'll find your
bank account mysteriously drained.

Hackers Homepage   www.hackershomepage.com

The place of choice for disgruntled sixteen-year-olds too spotty-looking to get served in pubs. Now in its sixth year and still proclaiming how legal it is. Great tips on phone freaking, code breaking and how to get a free satellite dish.

Icons Plus   www.iconsplus.com

Lots of PC and Mac icons to brighten up your computer. A very bright day for *Star Trek* fans.

The Illustrated Guide to   http://members.aol.com/
Breaking Your Computer   spoons1000/break

As if working in an office weren't stressful enough, a computer crash can be enough to turn the mildest-mannered employee into a raging psycho. If wanton destruction of office furniture is the only relief then this is the place to learn how to do it properly. If you're armed with household power tools and these instructions, keyboards, disks, monitors and hard drives won't have a hope.

Information Unlimited   www.amazing1.com

A New Hampshire corporation dedicated to the experimenter and technology enthusiast. This highly creative company holds many patents, ranging from weapons development to children's toys, and hopefully isn't planning on mixing them up.

Jargon   http://earthspace.net/jargon

If you feel you're showing your age by not being completely up to date with the latest hacking lingo then check out this handy glossary of hackers' terms.

Killer Fonts   www.killerfonts.com

This hardly blows apart the myth of computer geeks being socially inept sociopaths. For just twenty dollars you can buy computer fonts corresponding to the handwriting of your favourite serial killer. And they're all there: Charlie Manson, Jeffrey Dahmer, even our very own Jack the Ripper.

Soda Constructor   http://sodaplay.com/constructor

An opportunity for a bunch of nerds to show off. The soda constructor 'animates and edits two-dimensional models', which loosely translates as long-forgotten maths shapes coming to life and weirdly moving around the PC screen. The overall but unintentional result is that it looks as if someone's let loose a bunch of mad spiders.

Thingys on the Net   www.oink.com/thingys

A list of hundreds of links to devices connected to the web: cameras, robots, telescopes, pagers, etc.

Unsatisfactory Software   www.unsatisfactory.freeserve.co.uk

A company devoted to keeping alive the low-tech delights of the Sinclair Spectrum. Most fondly remembered is the Advanced Lawnmower Simulator. Anyone wanting to get back to their pre-acne geek glory days will love a nostalgic trip down this particular memory lane.

What Is It   http://core77.com/contraption/
Good For?   october/diskgame.html

Fine marketing has got AOL where it is today as the world's biggest ISP. The world is currently awash with those stupid little free-trial discs that always find their way into the bin eventually. This site allows people to submit the best ideas for alternative uses before their ultimate demise.

Where's George? Bill Locator   www.wheresgeorge.com

Unleashing the mighty potential of databases, this site is attempting to track the flow of dollar bills. If you're bored and sitting at work simply type in the serial numbers of any dollar bills that you have in your wallet and you may be lucky enough to be able to trace where they've been before they came into your possession. After recent news that just about every bill has traces of cocaine on it the one thing that's almost certain is that it's been up someone's nose.

24//SEX, DRUGS & ROCK'N'ROLL

The whole 'sex, drugs and rock'n'roll' thing is now so passé. The wild children of yesterday are now golf aficionados and even today's rock stars are company CEOs. But there's still plenty of interest in the naughty side of life.

Sex

Nobody would deny that there's a lot of sex out there on the web. Sure, some of it's unpleasant and nasty, but people wouldn't look at it if they didn't want to. In fact we owe porn sites quite a lot, because without them the web wouldn't have mushroomed into the beast that it's become today. The following, however, are a selection of porn-free websites.

Bedsit Dwellers and their Hoovers
http://opera.cit.gu.edu.au/bizarre/biz.084.html

Compelling (in a *Doctor Who*-behind-the-sofa-fashion) medical reports of tragic lone dwellers who sought sexual gratification in the form of the domestic dust buster.

Best Unintentionally Phallic Motel Sign
www.zdnet.com/yil/content/depts/billsbest/plaustin.html

The winner is the Austin Motel in Texas. 'I see this as a monument to twentieth-century humanity,' says the site's baffled owner Dottye Dean. 'A place where everyone can come together and feel welcome.' Not that welcome, presumably.

Cartoon Girls I Want to Nail
www.geocities.com/TelevisionCity/1356/

This is one web author who is at least honest. Too terrified to encounter the 'fairer sex', he's decided to post his thoughts on animated characters who get him going. He does add that he digs web porn as much as the next red-blooded guy though.

C-ya Relationship Closure Cards   www.c-ya.com
Terminate that tedious relationship with this specially designed range of cards. Apparently inspired by Oprah Winfrey, the self-help trend of the 90s, and the originator's personal growth.

Furniture Porn   www.vgg.com/furnporn1.html
If 'Hardcore furniture action' is your thing then this is the place to fantasise about your Queen Annes. In true interactive porn style there's even an opportunity to bid for your favourite bit of furniture.

Girlfriend Stealers Homepage   www.girlfriendstealer.com
Not, as expected, an opportunity for broken-hearted lovers to shop the immoral rat who stole the love of their lives. Instead a glorification of relationship wrecking that provides ample tips and advice on tearing apart even the happiest couples.

Ibrator   www.ibrator.com
Mac's trendy translucent colours have been copied for every household object. They've now found their way to tarting up marital aids. Teal or raspberry?

Kama Sooty   www.kama-sooty.co.uk
See Sooty and friends in various rude poses.

Love Ewe   www.muttonbone.com
For homesick Welshmen and Kiwis everywhere, or just the ultimate stag-night accessory (after the stripper), it's the inflatable sheep with integral wellie attachments. Through the powers of e-commerce one of these little lovelies will be discreetly delivered to your doorstep in a plain package.

Loving Links   www.lovinglinks.co.uk
For unhappily married people looking to play away from home without all the hassle of actually having to pick up a total stranger. Claiming to be a discreet extramarital dating service, this allows

people to avoid all of the tedious small talk and get straight down to the pants-dropping business.

Miss Jessup's Jesus Is Lord www.internettoilet.com/
Escort Service users/missjessup
Classy and discreet personal services for the discriminating pastor. A modern-day Mary Magdalene for the men of the cloth.

Pantycondoms http://birthcontrol.com/panty.html
Think again if safe sex means not removing your pants. Deranged scientists from Colombia have been in cahoots with their government to produce this unique form of contraception. Apparently the authorities in the United States are less than impressed.

Piece Together Last Night www.deepshock.co.uk
Somewhere through the booze-addled haze of your memories of last night you have the vague recollection of kissing someone and you find a strange phone number in your pocket. Should you take the risk? Potential bunny boiler or future spouse? This Romeo's Identikit will help you recover enough memory of the night before to make the right decision.

The Rules www.therulesbook.com
Tried and tested ways to trap men and lure them into marriage. Published in 27 languages to keep jewellers throughout the world in business.

Sex Quotes www.sexquotes.com
A unique service that combines two of the most sought-after commodities on the web, stock quotes and adult entertainment.

Sexual Records www.sexualrecords.com
Not Barry White, the other kind. Like *The Guinness Book of Records* for bedroom gymnastics. Bone up on which race is the best endowed or who was the deadliest female sadist in history.

Sexually Explicit   http://lynx.neu.edu/home/httpd/z/
Origami   zbrown/origami/underground
Excellent party tricks ahoy. Impress bored drunkards in the kitchen with dexterity from your digits.

The Shower Project   www.theshowerproject.com
The highly commendable endeavour of one overweight, middle-aged man to prove to his workmates that he wasn't gay. After overhearing gossip at work our hero decided to take pictures of himself in the shower with one hundred different women. All very tasteful – and they all look like very willing participants.

Tipper Gore's Guide to   www.geocities.com/
Dating Do's and Don'ts   CapitolHill/6806
Al Gore's wife is a renowned prude and all-round interfering busybody. Not content with stopping swearing on records, she wants to stop kids having sex. Read this before heading out.

Tips for Dating Emotional Cripples   www.grrl.com/bipolar.html
Girls who go for interesting guys who are interesting only on the surface – because they're in bands or are actors – often get disappointed when they're some way into the relationship. When super confidence is down to superego and selfishness they tend to be referred to as emotional cripples. This will provide invaluable advice for girls who persist in making their lives difficult.

Useless Sexual Trivia   http://useless-sex.com
Neither useless nor trivial: we didn't get here today without the help of sex – well, the majority of us anyway. So impress friends with little gems like the fact that both Hitler and Napoleon were lacking in the testicular department and that the word 'gymnasium' comes from the Greek word that means 'to exercise naked'. Or delight in their fascination as they hear that the banana slugs of the northwest end their thirty-hour hermaphroditic mating session by chewing off each other's male sex organs.

Virtual Flirt   **http://216.22.206.68/start.asp**
Cyber geeks can make up for the fact that they've been out of the
dating game for years by practising a few slick moves before they
head out. Pick your victim from a line-up of pub girls and throw them
a killer line from a number of suggestions. Pick the right one and that
lucky lady is on the fast track for bedroom bliss – in your dreams.

Way too personal   **www.waytoopersonal.com**
A first-hand look at Internet dating from someone who's been
there and done it. These are some of the replies to one woman's
ads. Anyone thinking of jumping into the web dating quagmire
needs to see this before they make their decision.

The Wonderful World of   **http://chimera.acs.ttu.edu/**
Gummy Bear Sex   **~emyrs/bears/bear.html**
Self-proclaimed 'Kama Sugar', multicoloured additive-laden
confectioneries get down and dirty with each other. All artistically
photographed in the best possible taste. Sticky fun for those with
special interests.

Drugs

*Sure, drugs are a problem, but they're not all bad and some of them
are even legal.*

Caffeine addiction quiz   **www.davesite.com/humor/caffeine**
If the thought of getting through the morning without copious
espressos is too hideous to contemplate, then coffee addiction
could be looming around the next corner. Self-diagnose with this
handy test.

Crack Aficionado   **www.thethirdrail.com/crack**
Satirical ezine about the joys of the rock. Those who object to not
being allowed to smoke in restaurants will be able to amuse
themselves with tales of Robert Downey Jr. and other addled
celebrities.

Designated Drinker — www.drunkenbastards.org/adb/ddlist/ddopen.htm

In the States getting legless and throwing up on the night bus just isn't an option, so one hapless friend has to endure their drunken friends for the evening and then suffer the torture of driving them home. This person is a designated driver and all groups of friends should have one. What's even more essential is the kind of friend that you can call up any time you fancy getting trashed and is guaranteed to want to join in. That particular hero is known as the Designated Drinker.

Dope Wars — www.beermatsoftware.com/dopewars/info.asp

Simple. Fun. Addictive. And that's just the game. Dope Wars is a role-playing game set in an imaginary drug market, which features dealing, pushing and evading the cops. Earn money and enter the Dealer Den and submit your highest balance.

420.com — www.420.com

If you're ever baffled by the kids squawking about 420s on American TV and ever wondered what they were going on about, then this is where the mystery is revealed. Four twenty is the not-so-secret calling code that US police use to signify that marijuana smoking is in progress. Just remember that this site doesn't in any way condone the use of illegal drugs. Yeah, right.

Kidstoned chewable Valium — www.retrogames.com/funstuff/kidstoned.mpg

What better way to keep hyperactive kids under control than junior sedatives? Kidstoned chewable Valium is a spoof TV ad done in wholesome fifties style. A must for all bleary-eyed parents.

Lip Balm Anonymous — www.kevdo.com/lipbalm/addict.html

A self-help group for people who find themselves with a physiological dependency for labial lubricant. There have to be worse things to find yourself addicted to, but any unfortunates struck down can use this as a starting point on the road to Betty Ford.

Little, Yellow, Different, Deadly www.martini.nu/rant/cyanide
If you're a compulsive party pill popper and the fizz has gone out of your life then cyanide could be the ultimate trip. With a handy symptom diagnosis chart to find out whether you're in need of this final dose.

Prozac Pez www.thegoodnamesweretaken.com/ProzacPez
Pez dispensers are undoubtedly the most stylish way ever invented of dispensing sweets. With the stresses of modern living causing people to pop Prozac as if they were mints, a Pez dispenser is the choicest way of administering a daily dose.

Psychoactive Toads www.erowid.org/animals/toads/toads.shtml
Cash-strapped Aussie hippies have long known of the effects of 5-hydroxy-N,N-dimethyltryptamine administered from the backs of *Bufo alvarius*. Or, to put it in plain English, they've been licking toads to get high. Anyone with a scientific interest should get the facts here.

Stoned .com www.stoned.com
All a bit Grateful Dead, really. Mesmerising psychedelic screens grace this site, which has no purpose or function other than to disorient rather than soothe. Hippie nonsense to waste away a few hours.

Tommy Chong's Urine Luck www.urineluck.com
Real-life products for hardworking corporate types with a secret life. Now that most US companies routinely dope-test their employees, there are other companies that will help people get through the test.

Virtual Crack www.virtualcrack.com
No more hanging around dark alleys with society's undesirables when your latest fix is a mere mouse click away. Virtual Crack is safe and clean, and won't get you arrested, even when you generously distribute it to friends.

Rock'n'roll

Music sites are ten a penny with their fancy MP3s and all those ways of avoiding having to buy a CD ever again. There are also a lot of people writing a lot of very funny things about the subject.

Backwards masking   http://gruel.spc.uchicago.edu/Backmask/music.html

They may have got away with those backward satanic messages on their records but those eighties heavy-metal bands were definitely guilty of bad hair, crap music and tight Lycra strides. Find out if some of the best-known hits of yesteryear get any better when they're played in reverse at The Complete Lyrics to 99 Bottles of Beer on the Wall (**www.virtual-media.com/vm/presents/ouzo/99bottles.html**). Life's too short? The very existence of The Complete Lyrics to 99 Bottles of Beer on the Wall is proof that for some life really is far too long. Typing out 2,414 words must be almost as pointless as counting them. Doh . . .!

A Brief History of Banned Music in the United States   http://ericnuzum.com/banned

There's a certain selection of the population who think music is as dangerous to an unformed mind as an atom bomb. This is one man's attempt to keep tabs on the censors.

Chaos Control Digizine   www.chaoscontrol.com

Alternative music ezine for the pierced and tattooed rock rebels out there.

Disco Vlad   www.zoetek.com/entrance/dancingcity

A Dutch version of the Village People, Carpenters' songs sung in Japanese, Abba sung in Hindi Disco . . . Vlad is a truly pan-cultural experience.

Electric Amish   www.electricamish.com
A band with a difference: three beardies armed with electric guitars
and a love of God and carpentry. It's hard to be entirely convinced
by the authenticity of their biographies.

Kiss This Guy   www.kissthisguy.com
It's always excruciating listening to people howling song lyrics,
especially when they haven't even got the decency to learn the
right words. This is an archive of the most popular misheard lyrics.

Large Hot Pipe Organ   www.lhpo.org
LHPO is 'the world's only MIDI-controlled, propane-powered
explosion organ', a terrifyingly powerful instrument. The only way
to make power music that would do justice to Wagner – with its
pyro-acoustic explodo-rhythmations throbbatising your earholes
and dance-ifying your booty to make you realise what industrial
music is all about.

Metal Sludge   www.metal-sludge.com
A metal magazine that's got a sense of humour. Particularly bizarre
is 'Donna's Domain', which features a collection of gossip and penis
ranking called 'The Long & Short of It', by the world-class crew-slut
Donna Anderson. For anyone into the boring music stuff there are
always reviews and all that other stuff.

Roadies   www.roadie.net
The unsung heroes of rock 'n' roll finally get their own place to
hang out. These tattooed road warriors are the people who keep
our highly strung musical heroes on the vaguely straight and
narrow.

Songs for Scouts   www.best.com/~michaele/Songs
Don't get your toggle in a twist any more. A wholesome collection
of good old campfire songs for the occasions when grown men
take a load of small children into the woods for the night.

Sum of Songs www.nctm.org/mt/2000/05/songs.html

One of the most thankless tasks imaginable has to be teaching maths to a bunch of bored kids. One teacher, Lawrence Mark Lesser, is trying to inject a little life into his numbers by 'making mathematics less monotone'. Just visualise this grown man standing in front of a class of teenagers rapping along to: 'Dividin' fractions, easy as pie. Flip the second and multiply! Multiplyin' fractions – no big problem. Top times top over bottom times bottom! When addin' fractions that you see. Match the bottoms perfectly!' Just the sort of thing to remind them of their dad's dancing at family weddings.

25//SHOPPING

The advent of secure online shopping has created thousands of new businesses. Everyone's heard of Amazon.com and their ilk, but more specialist items are also breaking into the public's consciousness. Products that people were in no danger of ever discovering are now freely available to anyone with a PC and a credit card. The Internet has spawned a truly global shopping centre and there are some truly bizarre things for sale.

Prêt à porter

While high street retailers have understandably shied away from online clothes shops, there's always room for the more specialist outfitter. Buying from the back of a magazine is rapidly becoming a thing of the past with 3D tours of clothing ranges and regular email updates about new product lines.

As Seen In   www.asseenin.com
Celebrity garb as seen on TV and movie screens. Find out exactly what those superstars are clad in and where to buy it.

Breastee   www.breastee.com
For the overadorned woman who's run out of spaces for more jewellery comes the Breastee. A unique and patented concept in cleavage adornment to cut a dash at the ambassador's party.

Bubblebodywear   www.bubblebodywear.com
Disposable air-filled plastic clothing for the discerning plastic fetishist. Now your pants can literally be filled with air. Beware: when you're standing at a bus stop the temptation for your fellow travellers to pop a few bubbles could be too much.

Hippy Skivvies
www.hippieskivvies.com

Remain true to those hippie roots in a corporate environment 'when ya gotta hide the hippie inside'. Not unwashed home helps, but a range of underwear that Jerry Garcia would have in glorious tie-dye. Surprisingly, it's made out of cotton, not hemp.

Mullet Wear
www.mulletwear.com

Show your derision of Satan's haircut with T-shirts, stickers and other merchandise. Should include a prize for the least suitable location for wearing any of the gear – an ice-hockey match, perchance?

Thunderwear
www.thunderwear.com

Skimpy underwear and automatic weapons may be great masturbatory fantasy fodder for the video industry, but where does the modern hot-pants-clad, gun-tottin' chick carry her piece? Down her trousers of course, but with the help of this genuine American-made pant holster.

Auctions

eBay, the online auction company, has really captured the public imagination with its bizarre offerings. From human kidneys to people's souls, and even their virginity, there's a whole bunch of websites that have sprung up just to keep track of the absurd lots posted. There's fearsome competition between these sites to spot the best of eBay, so check back regularly.

Bark
www.auctionrover.com/Bark

Spreads its wings a little further than eBay to include white-trash taxidermy, *Playboy* paraphernalia and psychedelic rock posters of the seventies.

Eday
http://eday.shutdown.com

Hits include deer-shit paperweights.

eWanted   www.ewanted.com
A slightly different spin: buyers post what they want and sellers bid
for it.

What the heck.com   www.whattheheck.com/ebay
Hits include really old toilet paper, the band Offspring and nails
from a serial killer.

Boy toys

---

*Men still young at heart hanker for the next gizmo to impress their
friends and bore their families. Since lad mags began to highlight
essential gadgets, many online retailers have sprung up to take
advantage of this affluent sector of the market.*

Aibo net   www.aibonet.com
To better the Tamagotchi craze, Sony have devised a ridiculously
expensive robot dog. Much cleaner than the real thing, and it
doesn't drop hairs or attack postmen unless you want it to. As
owners are unlikely to come across another one in the park, this
official homepage is the online meeting point.

Ceiva   www.ceiva.com
Why stare at the same picture over your mantelpiece all the time?
The Ceiva is the world's first Internet-connected picture frame for
sofa browsing.

Cheaper Than Dirt   www.cheaperthandirt.com
Quality firearms and weaponry at discount prices. The shop of
choice for maniacs everywhere whose next port of call is death or a
jail sentence.

Contraption   www.core77.com/contraption
A diverse monthly review of remarkable products such as table
lamps made out of straws and 3D cameras. All the products are

reviewed in a seemingly random way as they come to the attention of the reviewers.

Dollar discounter   www.dollardiscounter.com
For the truly mean. A spin on the online shopping mall that allows punters to buy a dollar's worth of credit for 95c.

FlyPower   www.flypower.com
For just $5.95 a pair, this is a lightweight glider powered by a housefly. Just trap a fly, calm it down by putting it in a freezer and then glue it to this contraption. Let it warm up and watch it fly the plane around until it croaks.

Force 10   www.force-ten.com
Get properly kitted out for a bit of revenge spying at Force 10 police and military supplies, because if you're not watching them, they're watching you.

Gulf Stream Pre-Owned   www.gulfstreampreowned.com
Forget trying to buy a car to impress your friends: get your hands on a second-hand jet and really make an entrance.

I Want One of Those   www.iwantoneofthose.com
Ultimate boy toys for the man who hasn't quite got everything. Sells everything from red phone boxes to MIG fighter jets.

Mpingo discs   www.shunmook.com/text1.htm
Serious hi-fi geeks are always trying to outdo each other with strange concepts to produce better sounds. Current king of the pointless gizmo is Mpingo discs, made from ebony and designed to be placed on equipment to tame any emanating resonance. For serious buffs only.

Nori the Original   www2.active.ch/
Nasal Passage Cleaner   ~gerstei
Claiming to be a natural and powerful way to help fight against colds, chronic headaches, earaches and insomnia. The Nori is

probably available in a solid-gold rock-star edition for serious party powder overindulgers in danger of losing their noses.

Personal www.ussubs.com/Luxury_folder/
Submarines lux.discov.html

If aquatic showing off is more your thing then check out the Discovery 1000, a state-of-the-art submersible that offers panoramic viewing and contemporary styling. Very important when trying to impress shoals of fish or going for that James Bond entrance to a party.

'Robokoneko' www.genobyte.com/
(Kitten Robot) robokoneko.html

Not to be outdone by Sony (see 'Aibo net' above), creative cat owners have retorted with a Robokoneko, which translates as robot child cat. Apparently, it contains a billion artificial neurones. Bet it still can't fetch a stick.

Small Parts www.smallparts.com

Tiny tools and accessories for building small things. Presumably frequented by Santa's little helpers.

Solotrek www.solotrek.com

This is the real James Bond look: a vertical-takeoff-and-landing exoskeletal flying vehicle. Handy for quick getaways and commuting.

Stadium Pal www.stadiumpal.com

Finally, the problem of missing half the game through toilet trips and drinking copious amounts of beer during a football game has been solved. The previous options were wetting yourself (embarrassing), taking a leak on the person in front of you (dangerous) or a sly one at the side of the stand ($136 disorderly-conduct fine in the US). The Stadium Pal is a wearable device to bring relief without anyone knowing.

Zorb www.zorb.com

A truly surreal form of travel. If you're rolling down a hill in a giant, transparent plastic ball then the chances are that you're travelling in a Zorb. Apparently it was designed for people who think *The Dukes of Hazzard* was the best show on TV, people who still remember *The Prisoner* from the first time around, people who can get ready in two minutes and people who take over an hour just to go to the supermarket.

Animal products

It's possible to buy some really specialised animal products, and the reasons for doing so couldn't be more diverse. The following are unlikely to be spotted next to the hamsters in your local pet shop. The question has to be asked about what kind of society will sustain a coyote urine or giraffe manure delivery business.

Dog Doo www.dogdoo.com

This company specialises in sending primo dog doo to hapless victims.

Glowdog www.glowdog.com

If you want to stop your favourite pet being flattened by a bus this winter, then ignore the humiliation and dress him up in something from Glowdog, the specialists in reflective wear for dogs and cats. Yes, people will laugh at your Derek Day-Glo hound when you go walkies, but do you really care?

Horse Turd in a Box http://home.earthlink.net/~inabox

Interflora's not much use when you want to demonstrate your disgust for someone who's riled you recently. What the world has been crying out for is equine manure delivery. It's even possible to choose the texture and weight of this most peculiar present.

Mutluks   www.muttluks.com
If you were mistakenly under the impression that thousands of years of evolution had equipped all but the most pathetic pooches with the necessary footwear for walking, then you'd be wrong. Mutluks think differently and want you to dress your doggie in their canine boots.

100% Predator Urines   www.predatorpee.com
Put the fear of god into the neighbourhood's king tomcat with some pee from way higher up the food chain. Tailor-made solutions for the area's problem animal featuring urine from coyotes, foxes, bobcats and wolves.

Poop Moose   www.poopmoose.com
Alaskan-made novelty sweet dispenser cum executive toy. Lift the head and it leaves a little deposit. Visitors to the office will be so impressed.

ZooDoo   www.zoodoo.com
Gardening hotshots not content with growing their flora with normal manure now have another option. Zoos are now selling exotic animal fertiliser for upmarket horticulturists. When only premium elephant or giraffe crap is good enough for those prize blooms, get in touch with these guys.

Consumer culture

The problem with all this ravenous acquisition of consumer products is that people have to deal with the customers. Not always the most pleasant of tasks, and sometimes it's downright dangerous. Then they complain when they can't keep hold of their precious items . . .

Customers Suck   www.customerssuck.com/index2.html
Retail therapy may be a great Saturday afternoon pastime but the poor wretches behind the tills know the pain that comes from

prolonged contact with the great unwashed. This, then, is the place shop workers go to whinge when the customer isn't always right.

Inconspicuous   **http://homearts.com/depts/**
Consumption   **pl/incosumr/00incoc1.htm**
An obsessive look at the stuff we take for granted, such as who makes that weird device they use to measure your foot at the shoe shop or who needs aerosol body glue. An excellent way of overloading on useless trivia.

Return Me.com   **www.returnme.com**
Tag personal stuff with coded labels. If anything's left in a cab and it's picked up by a good Samaritan, all they have to do for a reward is to give Fed Ex a ring. They'll then pick it up and return it to its rightful owner.

Shop In Private   **www.shopinprivate.com**
People too timid to scream across a busy pharmacy that their anal warts have erupted can shop here with confidence. Embarrassment-free shopping for most socially compromising ailments.

Thrift Store   **www.cpsc.gov/cpscpub/**
Safety Checklist   **pubs/thrift/thrftck.html**
A recent study of US thrift stores revealed that an estimated 69 per cent of the stores were selling at least one type of hazardous consumer product. Be prepared for the perils of second-hand clothing.

Trivial Customer   **http://204.251.21.22/cgi-bin/**
Complaints   **complaints/most_recent_complaints.cgi**
Lowbrow genuine complaints. Companies should feel sorry enough for these people to help them out.

Unclaimed Baggage Center   **www.unclaimedbaggage.com**
A genuine outlet store in Alabama. When people don't claim their bags, these people do and then clean up the clothes and sell the lot.

What they should do is operate a lucky-dip service for people to buy unopened bags.

Shocking fillers

There are some products that you'd never spot in any shop even if you lived to be two hundred. Now that shopping on the web is a day-to-day reality, some of the most bizarre things are just a mouse click away. These items are unlikely to end up in the nation's stockings this Christmas.

Archie McPhee   **www.mcphee.com**
Anyone looking for a deluxe rubber chicken or a cockroach lunchbox need look no further than this mad little shop in Seattle, Washington. Bonkers stuff guaranteeing that no one will ever buy the same presents that you do.

Biblical Plague Waterdomes   **www.plaguedomes.com**
Ultimate revenge presents for those irritating relatives who insist on showering you with annoying, cutesy little shake-'em-up snow scenes. In fact, even better than that, collect the set for yourself and make sure they never come to visit.

Biotoy   **www.biotoy.com**
Handy stockist of glow-in-the-dark water pistols and alien crystals. Biotoy is the online store for bioluminescent toys and games that glow in the dark.

Buy My In-laws   **www.geocities.com/BourbonStreet/9319**
Take my mother-in-law, literally. With gift wrapping and delivery options plus all the associated accessories, this should be one e-business going down the pan very soon.

Corpses For Sale   **http://distefano.com**
For those situations when a fake corpse just won't do, buy a real one. From Lady Die to Nazi Zombies, this place has the lot.

Disgustoscope   www.eskimo.com/%7Ebillb/
                                      amateur/dscope.html

The opposite of a kaleidoscope: instead of making pretty patterns it produces a real-life, 3D horror movie. A bad Christmas present but a great way of traumatising loud kids.

Gobler Toys   www.goblertoys.com/pages/toys.html

It's a miracle that the Baby Boomers made it this far. A selection of unwholesome sixties toys from an age before health warnings were invented. It's not hard to see why play-dead coffins and battery-powered smell amplifiers never caught on.

**Los Angeles County Coroner's
Office Gift Shop**   . www.lacoroner.com

Is nothing sacred from the spread of commercialisation? Old Quincy certainly wouldn't approve of Skeletons in the Closet, the gift shop of the LA coroner. Gruesome presents include a personalised toe tag (don't we all get them eventually?), or miniature skulls – all in the worst possible taste.

Meaniebabies   www.meaniebabies.com

Twisted toys including the Infamous range: Dennis Rodmantis, Jerry Stinger, Mick Jaguar and Mallard Stern. Particularly good are Dopeymon, the bald No Fur-be and Teletushy.

Planet Love   www.planet-love.com

A perennial favourite of computer programmers everywhere. When antisocial working hours and personal hygiene prevent forging meaningful relationships, get an off-the-peg service from this company, who provide mail-order brides from around the world.

Pull My Finger   www.fartcd.com

Scatological humour for the office joker in us all, a CD of genuine farts. The novelty value would last for . . . seconds.

Ruby Montana's Pinto Pony   www.rubymontana.com

Got a thing for cheesiness and can't quite make it to Seattle? The high priestess of kitsch has kindly put her emporium up on the web for cyber visitors to peruse. From Spam carving to Elvis shrine kits, the seventies live on.

Stupid.com   www.stupid.com

The place to buy stupid things. Stupid candy, stupid gifts, stupid jokes and stupid games.

The Fart Filter   www.fartypants.com/fartfilter.html

Foul-arsed colleagues can be neutralised using military-grade technology designed to protect troops from nerve-gas attacks. Claims to provide a 'ring of confidence' to those who have had too much of everything. An activated charcoal pant pad will calm the impact of the most filthy eruptions. Mail-ordered to your doorstep in a brown-paper parcel for a mere fiver.

26//SPORT

The world of sport isn't confined to *Grandstand* and Saturday afternoons. The Internet is a breeding ground for the out-of-the-ordinary sporting quest. Football and rugby seem quite mundane pastimes compared with elephant polo and fire diving. Getting fit and making friends have never been so bizarre.

Balf   **www.balf.com**
Balf was invented in 1994 almost certainly as a result of over-indulgence in something. A game that manages to combine baseball and golf and upsets the worst-dressed group of people on the planet can't be all bad. Anyone looking for membership of their local course would be well advised to check whether it's been banned.

Belt Sander Drag Racing   **www.beltsander-races.com**
With every self-respecting yuppie going for the nouveau-poor, stripped-floorboard look at the moment, it was inevitable that some less-than-willing participants would let their minds wander. Next time you find yourself on all fours, covered in dust with a power tool between your legs, think of it as training for the Grand Prix of the International Belt Sander Drag Race Association.

Bog   **www.kudos.co.uk/15mins/**
Snorkelling   **Issue6/bogsnork.html**
It would probably do the enthusiasts of this hobby a favour if people visited this website and told the owners why diving in the Caribbean is an altogether preferable experience to moving through a Welsh bog wearing a snorkel and mask.

Buzkashi   **www.afghan-web.com/**
                                          sports/buzkashi.html
You've got to be tough as old boots to live in Afghanistan, as their national sport will testify. Literally translated as 'goat grabbing', it's

polo played with a goat carcass. Now that cattle are becoming more plentiful they're using them. Extreme.

Elephant Polo   www.tigermountain.com/WEPA

A truly macho sport if ever there was one. This is the official World Elephant Polo Association website. Quite how anyone can steer an elephant around a hockey pitch is anyone's guess, but these bizarre sportsters seem to manage it.

Fielding's danger finder   www.fieldingtravel.com/df

If extreme sports are your thing and you laugh in the face of fear, maybe you should up the ante with Fielding's danger finder. A compendium of some of the places to do things that you may never return from.

Fire Diving   http://home.netcom.com/~time2div/fire1.html

Once you're bitten by the extreme sports bug, life becomes just a long search for more potentially suicidal kicks. Stop searching because the sport to end all sports has arrived: fire diving. The idea is to get yourself scooped up in one of those huge water buckets that helicopters fill up before dumping them on forest fires. The reason why is anyone's guess.

Noodling   www.theatlantic.com/issues/
97feb/catfish/catfish.htm

Possibly not the most dangerous or extreme form of fishing but almost certainly one of the daftest. The idea is to use yourself for fishing bait. Simply stick your hand into a catfish's lair, wait for the bite, stick your fingers down his throat and wrestle it to dry land.

Radical and Extreme Hobbies   http://reh42.com/asubject

Combining life-threatening danger and huge expenditure on toys, this could for many men be the ultimate hobby site. All things high-powered, fast, loud, exploding and fire-breathing including nitrous scooters, hot rods and home rockets. Book your cemetery lot now.

Recently Released Names

It can't be that easy to find an original and witty name for racehorses nowadays. The US Jockey Club recycles names by releasing the competition monikers of deceased nags. About fifty thousand this year alone.

Swamp Buggy Racing
www.swampbuggy.com

Aquatic drag racing with thousand-horsepower deathtraps. Probably one of the best ways to escape from the murderous, inbred natives.

The Chicken Wing Bet
www.chickenwingbet.com

Two friends chomping on chicken wings during a football game made a wager for the rest of the season based on what they were eating. After that, it seemed like a good idea to set up their own sports betting site with a difference. Money doesn't change hands – just their favourite snack.

321CYA Productions
www.321cya.com

Like the idea of base jumping from the comfort of your living room? For armchair scaredy-cats comes a series of loony jumping videos. All endorsed with the completely sane 'Buy these videos or I'll shoot my cat' tagline.

Tractor Pulling
www.tractorpulling.com

A virtual hoedown for all nose-pickin', 'shine-swillin', sister-marryin' hicks is the European Tractor Pulling Website, which partially explains why Scandinavians turbocharge their tools and tow blocks of concrete in front of their families and friends.

27//STRANGE BODIES

There's no use denying that there's a lot of flesh on the web. Even when porn sites are taken out of the equation there's still plenty to go around. People just can't be stopped from showing themselves off or collecting pictures of odd-looking people and laughing at them.

Born natural

Some people get in a lather about the strangest things. There are some very strange and harmless fetishes out there based on the most innocuous characteristics. Others just love their own bods and just want to share them with the rest of the world.

Boob Scan - **www.boobscan.com**
The saucier version of the infamous Cat Scan site (see 'The Cat Scan Contest' on page 155. Rather than press innocent moggies on to a scanner screen, users are invited to press their mammaries. Makes photocopying your bum at the office Christmas party seem a tad tame.

Gap Toothed **www.gap-toothed.com**
Everyone needs a little space according to these people, who are celebrating their goofyness. Don't feel like an orthodontic outcast ever again after browsing through the lists of celebrities who share your predicament.

LiquidPoop **www.liquidpoop.com**
A bizarre attempt to remove the shame and stigma of diarrhoea through poetry. Quite why people would want to do this is anyone's guess. 'Darling, let me serenade you with this ode I wrote to the squits' doesn't seem to be the perfect material for iambic pentameter, but it takes all sorts.

The Long Hair Site www.tlhs.org

One gentleman's passion for ladies who wear their hair very long. Whether he really likes this kind of thing or not is open to question, because he seems to be earning a bit of spare cash by flogging off CD-ROMs of previous editions of the site.

Mingers www.mingers.com

Only their mothers could love them. This is the home of the facially inept, and it's a cruel gallery of photos of folk who'll never be partying with the beautiful people.

Navels International and www.tigerx.com/
Celebrity Bellybuttons bbs

Now the nombril has replaced the cleavage as the flesh of choice for the right-on woman to flash, here comes the world's first non-rude porn site. Navels International and Celebrity Bellybuttons is a celebration of those odd little tummy indentations, with results of voting for the world's most sexy.

The Twisted Lens www.twistedlens.com

A showcase for the work of a San Francisco-based artist who takes pictures of girls wearing glasses. Maybe they're too myopic to figure that he's a bit strange.

The Voluntary Human Extinction Movement www.vhemt.org

We all know that Earth is becoming a smelly overcrowded place and that soon we're not going to be able to produce enough food for the world's burgeoning population. This group of people propose an ethical way of reducing human numbers, unlike a number of twentieth-century dictators.

Not satisfied with what they were given

Sometimes what you were born with just isn't enough and there's a proliferation of sites out there dedicated to altering your appearance.

Billy Bob Teeth   **www.billy-bob-teeth.com**

Swamp chic for $10. Get some inbred orthodontics with these horrific falsies. Just added to the product range: Austin Powers gnashers.

Body Modification Ezine   **www.bme.com**

Anyone who thinks that bod mods stop at tattoos and the odd navel piercing should think again and visit this site. Arguably a collection of some of the most extreme body changes. Some of these 'improvements' are definitely not for the faint of heart.

Men With Moustaches   **www.moustache.de/starte.htm**

A place where men who look like something out of Village People hang out. If you're a believer in the claim that handlebars exist best under your nose then this is your kind of place.

The Nipple Project   **www.cultofmarms.org**

The owner of this project claims that due to circumstances beyond her control she has found herself in need of new nipples. Lacking the scientific know-how to design them for herself, she is using this website to ask people to help her by submitting ideas of their own.

What Happens   **www.cirp.org/library/**
During Circumcision?   **procedure/plastibell**

If you thought that it's all snip, snip, ow!, followed by tears and you're not sure whether to put your newborn through it, then it's possible to do a bit of research. This educational video will reveal all.

Mullets

Ever since the Beastie Boys penned a little ditty to the mighty mullet hairdo, they've become something of a web and cultural phenomenon. Like a post-Holocaust cockroach, the mullet is the haircut that refuses to die. In spite of being universally derided by every medium, this coiffured monstrosity shows no sign of extinction and is currently living a healthy existence in US trailer parks, ice hockey rinks and Germany. There are thousands of mullet sites out there, but these are the best.

Mullet Frenzy   **www.mulletfrenzy.com**

New home of the infamous Mullet Research Expedition, an out-in-the-field mullet investigation. Where daring photographers risk life and limb to snap the real-life mullets in their natural habitats.

Mullets Galore   **www.mulletsgalore.com**

This is undoubtedly the king of all mullet sites. Painstaking research has gone into categorising every type of mullet and tracking down examples of their kind. The aggressive quality and the type of person likely to be wearing one is even speculated upon. A masterpiece.

The North American   **www.geocities.com/**
Mullet Page   **Hollywood/Hills/6906**

Examining the main exponents of the American ice hockey hair cut. Particularly good celebrity section.

28//THE CYCLE OF LIFE

Children, work, marriage and death. It don't matter who you are, but most of these things are inescapable for the majority of people.

Children

Proud parents showing off their newborns doesn't have the greatest scope for comedy appeal. They all look like Winston Churchill and Mummy and Daddy are just so proud. Nevertheless . . .

The law of the playground www.log.dial.pipex.com/playground

Kids can be so evil. If you don't know the schoolyard lingo, you're guaranteed a good kicking. Refresh memories with little gems like BO Baracus and Vaseline Boy.

The Society for Preventing Parents from Naming Their Children Jennifer www.gizmo1.demon.co.uk/jencyclo/data/sppntcj.htm

With more and more American kids being named Jennifer, national confusion is imminent. One group of concerned citizens is intent on stopping this mad craze before it's too late.

Work

Most people spend more time at work than they do sleeping. Nobody really wants to be there and their fate is almost entirely in the hands of management with questionable ability. It's no surprise, then, that there's plenty of healthy humour about the workplace on the web. After all, most of it is specifically catering for the millions of bored people sneaking a sly peek from their workplace PC.

Co-workers' Hints   www.coworkerhints.com
Navigate that moral minefield of co-workers with bad personal
hygiene, particularly bad breath, body odour or flatulence. Should
they be tactfully approached? Of course not: send money to this
company and they'll write your nasty letter.

Dangerous Jobs   www.fieldingtravel.com/df/dngrjobs.htm
A timely reminder that most people's lot isn't that bad after all.
Work may be boring, but at least there's a fair chance of making it
home at night.

Do I Work With   www.angelfire.com/ca2/
a Serial Killer?   tacoswaste/killer.html
Cruel office workers have decided that they're working with a mass
murderer. You decide from their evidence and help persecute this
poor unfortunate.

Dumb Boss   www.dumbboss.com
Share contempt for the boss with like-minded individuals with this
collection of real-life stories. Bosses, do you recognise any of the
stories?

I Resign.com   www.i-resign.com
Instead of sitting at your desk all day seething with hatred for your
boss, just quit and work somewhere else. The resignation portal has
all the information the potential leaver is ever going to need, from
how to write the letter to suing the company, and a bit of light-
hearted humour to take some of the heat out of this stressful
situation.

Litigation-Proof   www.wildcowpublishing.com/
Letters of Recommendation   other/letter.html
Most employers don't realise that those glowing letters of
recommendation that they write when the office pest is finally a
distant memory can come back and haunt them. Rather than being
sued for landing some incompetent on another organisation, learn

how to be economical with the truth and avoid any messy comebacks.

My Boss   www.myboss.com

They earn too much money, pretend they're always working and shout too much. A sly chance to get even with the guy who's next in the pecking order. Rammed with crazy quotes and insane anecdotes.

9–5 Café   www.9to5cafe.com

While away hours of boredom with games such as 'Shoot the Boss'. Knowing exactly where their target audience have come from, the considerate people behind this site have furnished each game with a panic button that restores the screen to an innocent-looking spreadsheet or word-processor document.

Random Letter of Resignation   www.underemployed.com/
Generator   fun_resignation.shtml

If you really don't care about your boss's feelings, just fire off a random resignation letter from underemployed.com. They'll be happy to help you spot and cope with a dead-end job. Best of all is learning how to antagonise the boss without getting into trouble. A skill to be mastered by every disgruntled employee.

The Simulator   www.conceptlab.com/simulator

A patronising way of finding out what it's like to flip burgers at McDonald's without the danger of getting covered in spots. Just follow the instructions.

Virtual Manager   www.virtual-manager.com

As if a real one weren't bad enough, there's another one to keep on screen for the whole day. Simply hit the button for more management *non-sequiturs*.

Marriage

Websites have been an instant hit with married couples. No more spending a fortune on costly photo reprints for absent guests when a simple website will suffice. There are literally thousands of proud couples who set up sites to share their happiness with their family and friends. Unfortunately, anyone can look at them, which can provide an endless source of amusement to anyone with a wicked sense of humour.

And the   **www.visi.com/~dheaton/**
Bride Wore   **bride/the_bride_wore.html**

Brides always look beautiful, glowing and delighted on their wedding day, right? Well not strictly. After putting so much effort into their looks, they can sometimes lose sight of the fact that they look ridiculous. Have a laugh at the expense of this collection of bridal atrocities that will haunt them for the rest of their lives.

Las Vegas Wedding Pranks   **www.pranks4thememories.com**

One crazy office prankster's hobby is to play pranks at his friends' weddings. The antics of this wacky guy are chronicled here. Presumably he's devoid of any teeth and has permanent black eyes.

A Wedding   **www.vegasinfo.com/vegas/**
with Elvis   **graceland_chapel.html**

For the wedding to piss off your parents until their dying days, jet off to Las Vegas and get married in the Graceland Wedding Chapel by an Elvis impersonator. Full price list and list of optional extras make it sound a lot more classy than half freezing to death in a cold church in Wolverhampton.

Ain't No Way To Go   www.aarrgghh.com/no_way
One man's compendium of the various ways people have departed this sphere of existence: some humorous, some horrific, all intriguing. It's a strange hobby, comprising a collection of news and magazine articles collected over the past two decades.

Darwin Awards   www.darwinawards.com
A web institution, and easily the best site with a death theme. The Darwin Awards celebrate Charles Darwin's theory of evolution by commemorating the remains of those who contributed to the improvement of our gene pool by removing themselves from it. The stories are absolutely jaw-droppingly staggering. Were there ever some dumb people out there!

DeadPool.org   www.deadpool.org
This is an annual event, where members compete to see who is the most skilful at predicting the most celebrity deaths. A bit like that old favourite office game to while away the post-New Year depression.

Death By Curry   www.geocities.com/NapaValley/6654
One man's quest to discover a curry so hot that he would be rendered lifeless on the spot. Basically a collection of recipes compiled within the guidelines of a dubious cult known as the 'Ring of Fire'. Worryingly, the pages haven't been updated recently. Maybe he hit the jackpot.

The Death Clock   www.deathclock.com
The Death Clock is the Internet's friendly reminder that life is slipping away. Just input your details and it'll tell you when you're going to expire. How short life is!

The electric chair www.theelectricchair.com

After a gruesome visit to New York State's electric chair, a grisly tourist and his brother made their own film about their trip. Since then they've expanded our horizons to include the death penalty, Andy Warhol, lightning, electrocution, Stephen King, electroshock therapy and other related phenomena of our wired society.

4Obituaries www.4obituaries.4anything.com

Recent deaths, best epitaphs, celebrity obituaries, and all things gruesome. Find out which celebrities died in air crashes.

Get a Life http://members.aol.com/
After Death ramces/rame01.htm

Immortality has been a human obsession since the dawning of time. The best we've come up with is some pretty suspect cryogenic companies who promise they'll thaw us out when they've worked out how to cure whatever it is that caused us to croak. German Frank Kempelmann offers a fresh perspective on immortality. Simply follow his nine-thousand-step recipe. Take one teaspoon of your body cells, one tablespoon of paraffin to preserve them, 1,000,000,000,000,000 bytes of computer space, 950 hours of spare time – and hey presto!

Memorialise a Loved One www.funerals-online.com

Funerals-OnLine is the website for a funeral partner. Swap crow-featured old men in black for a chirpy website and funerals suddenly seem a lot more depressing. Still, it's the future for everyone.

The National Museum of Funeral History www.nmfh.org

What a fun day out for all the family! Traipse around this place and just watch the children as they start sobbing and moaning. Presumably does a swift trade from passing goths who must treat this as some sort of national shrine.

The Online Suicide Note   www.mindseye.net/~sharp11/Suicide
Good news for the terminally depressed and lethargic. The Online Suicide Note will compose a final missive for the virtual illiterati without the bother of having to string a whole sentence together.

The Celebrity Dead Pool   www.stiffs.com
The original site to see who's croaked from the world of entertainment and sport. A bit like a virtual graveyard except that the staff mock the deceased.

Viewlogy   www.leif.com
For some grieving relatives a headstone and an epitaph just don't do justice to their dear departed. In America, surprisingly enough, there's a company that will go way beyond a tombstone photo. They'll electronically store and display on the stone the person's entire life story in words and photos. This could prompt a whole new ghoulish craze for trainspotters – Sunday afternoons may never be the same.

Wills on the Web   www.ca-probate.com/wills.htm
Nobody's really interested in the hand-me-downs of old timers like Samuel Johnson and Ben Franklin, but have you ever wondered what Elvis or John Lennon left behind and for whom? This is a collection of some interesting wills that expand your trivia knowledge and could impress people in a number of social situations.

Wow, What a Way To Go   www.wowwhatawaytogo.com
Cremation with attitude and style. 'Phoenix Rising' will provide artists and scatterers to create a truly unique ash-disposal service from 'Fireworks' to 'Sea Planes', 'Helicopters' to 'Hot Air Balloons' and 'Rocketing Into Space'. Be an individual until the very end.

29//THE WEB ITSELF

The Internet had a fairly profound impact on late-twentieth-century culture. With smarmy dotcom whiz kids and crippling email viruses, the net became both the bête noir and savoir of the media. It's definitely changed office culture, shopping, humour and entertainment, and a whole culture and etiquette have sprung up around net use.

The Anti-Chain Letter   www.perry.com/bizarre/antichn.html
Blitz those annoying people forever sending chain letters with the ultimate of its kind. A bizarre, meandering rant that will confuse and amuse. Guaranteed to make people think before hitting that send button.

Blowthedotoutyourass.com   www.blowthedotoutyourass.com
The backlash to smug dotcom millionaires is well under way with this anti-web-company site. Fantastic stickers available, containing anti-web-culture slogans.

Braille   http://members.tripod.com/
website   ~bannerland/braille.htm
Touchy feely site for the visually impaired, although no explanation of how they're supposed to get there.

Create Your Own Hoax   www.cao.com/hoax
Those irritating chain emails that make you think you'll be cursed if they don't get forwarded to everyone you've ever met have to start somewhere. This is the place: just follow the instructions to start one of your own.

The Empty Website   http://emptywebsite.com
A haven of Zen-like tranquillity in the middle of overpopulated web chaos. Just calm nothingness.

Forward Garden www.forwardgarden.com

Where those faintly amusing office emails go to die. Alternatively, be the person in your office to start one off. Hundreds to choose from.

Fucked Company www.fuckedcompany.com

After the success of the Dead Pool game (see page 197) and with the imminent bursting of the dotcom bubble comes the inevitable dotcom dead pool.

Great 404s of the Web www.plinko.net/404/area404.asp

The benchmark of geekiness is to actually know what a 404 is. For those fortunate enough not to know, it's the boring page that comes up when you hit a broken link, telling you that you've hit a broken link. This is a collection of personalised 404s divided into categories, including cool, funny, interactive and strange.

Internet Scambusters www.scambusters.com

The web is only now shaking off its dodgy reputation as a place where people are robbed of their hard-earned cash. Internet Scambusters tirelessly works to reveal these crooks to the world.

Internet Squeegee Guy www.website1.com/squeegee

Nowadays the only socially acceptable time to refer to the Internet as the Information SuperHighway is in parody scenarios. Like any major thoroughfare, the ISH has its own lowlife made up from the socially disadvantaged.

The Internet Beggar www.irational.org/skint

Any of us could be on the skids like this poor creature one day. Like his street-dwelling counterpart, he will harangue you, but there's no need to fumble for loose change. With just one secure online transaction you can pay him by credit card and he'll say 'God bless ya, sir'.

The Internet License   www.webreference.com/
Plate Gallery   outlook/license/gallery.html

Silicon Valley madness. Be a geek and be proud of it. A collection of photos of number plates of cars owned by computer types who just want to shout about what they do for a living.

The Last Page of   www.wackycreations.com/
the Internet   lastpage.html

As they say, 28 words on a web page, no frills, no graphics. Simply announcing that the visitor has reached the very last page of the Internet and that they should now go outside and play.

Meta Spy   www.metaspy.com

Find out what the world is searching those engines for. This site reveals the most looked-for things on the web. Obviously the rude 'Exposed' one is the one to go for.

Oh My   www.ohmygoodness.com/
Goodness   Cards/viagra-big.jpg

The social implications of a flaccidity cure that doesn't rely on consuming the appendages of the world's endangered animals are still being assessed. The web is awash with a flood of Viagra jokes and this site excels in the provision of electronic postcards based around this hot topic. In particular, it has the best saucy seaside-style big-V parodies for the times when the only thing you can't manage is to make it to the post box.

The Shredder   www.potatoland.org/shredder

Redundant websites should be recycled, not binned. Pop them into the digital shredder to add to digital landfill.

Smilies   www.smilies.com

It soon becomes obvious when you're dealing with an Internet veteran. Their chat-room antics and emails are peppered with baffling abbreviations and acronyms, and those weird little bunched-up brackets and dots. They're called smilies and they're supposed to denote light-hearted friendliness, but they just make people seem like nerds. This is a collection of just about all the ones that anyone's ever thought of.

Total Obscurity   **www.totalobscurity.com**
The page you can find only by accident – one man's inane rantings.

Web Economy   **www.dack.com/web/**
Bullshit Generator   **bullshit.html**
This would be hilarious if it weren't so true. It's an essential pre-meeting browse just to spot how many of these nonsensical lines are uttered in all seriousness by some jumped-up corporate climber. Just keep hitting the button to simulate the dread felt in those interminable meetings.

The Yuckiest Site on the Internet   **www.nj.com/yucky**
Obviously isn't, but when Lego loses its appeal rug rats will be captivated by this site's investigation of bodily fluids and the hours of fun that can be had with them.

30//THINGS TO TRY

The web is a never-ending source of enlightenment, crammed with loads of new things to broaden your intellectual horizons. The following sites will fail to broaden anything and could result in a hospital visit.

Don't try this at home

Some things that your mum would probably tell you not to do. Maybe vegetating on the sofa wasn't such a bad idea after all.

Banja   **www.banja.com**
A curiously addictive game where players get to be Banja, then Rasta, who finds himself shipwrecked and has to come to terms with the strange inhabitants of a desert island. At times you get to jump into other characters to interact with all the other players in this marooned community.

Blow Up a Gerbil   **www.joecartoon.com/**
in a Microwave   **download/dlgerbil.html**
Virtual rodent rage. It's a cartoon – no gerbils were really harmed in the making of this amusing little tale. But if you've ever wondered . . .

The Booger Page –   **www.cybersim.com/**
Digging for Gold?   **booger/default.htm**
Indispensable tips for that thorny issue of mucus disposal to retain a little dignity at the next social event.

Build Some Boogers   **www.youcan.com/mucus/mucus.html**
If you've ever examined the end of your finger after a good dig and wondered what snot is made of, your quest is over. With the aid of a microwave oven and some standard kitchen products you can whip up as much as you like.

Cards As   **http://students.db.erau.edu/**
Weapons   **~weddj/yatz.html**
It's actually a book that the owner of this site found by accident one day, and he was so totally overcome with the concept that he wants to tell the world about it. For the poker samurai in us all, or even the perpetual loser.

Creative Answering Machine   **http://albrecht.ecn.purdue.edu/**
Messages   **~taylor/humor/answering.html**
Banish that stock monotone greeting with some slightly more creative ways of embarrassing callers.

Fun with Grapes –   **www.sci.tamucc.edu/**
A Case Study   **~pmichaud/grape**
Grape racing is cheap post-pub fun that requires only a microwave oven, cooking oil and some grapes. Follow the instructions for some very cheap thrills. Even better, get drunk enough to deny everything in the morning and refuse to clean the microwave oven.

The Great Canadian   **www.geocities.com/SouthBeach/**
Grape Race   **Marina/7632/grape.html**
Grapes. A plate. Some oil. A microwave. All the ingredients you need for a really good night in.

Jamming a Pair of Scissors   **www.armchair.mb.ca/**
Repeatedly Into Your Crotch   **~scissors**
Unique individuals under the impression that they would for ever have to partake solo will be consoled by learning of all the celebrities who partake in their little hobby. Know you're in good company the next time you reach for the scissors.

Perpetual Bubblewrap!   **www.urban75.com/Mag/bubble.html**
When the real thing is scarce the Internet is at hand. Simply roll the mouse over the bubble wrap to see and hear a satisfying 'pop' as the bubble bursts.

Piercing Mildred   **www.mildred.com**
Apparently a combination of two of the nineties' favourite pastimes – body modification and the Internet. Piercing Mildred offers the chance to exact body modifications such as exotic tattoos, piercings and scarification without all the mess and pus. It's actually just an online game, but there's a chance to come into contact with some other piercing freaks.

Strawberry Pop-Tart   **www.sci.tamucc.edu/**
Blow-Torches   **~pmichaud/toast**
Strawberry pop tarts can be used as inexpensive incendiary devices. Take a box of pop tarts and a toaster and just follow the instructions. Probably a good idea to keep a phone to hand for the inevitable call to the fire brigade.

Stuff the Warning Label   **www.ittc.ukans.edu/~botanika/**
Said Not to Do   **warning_label.htm**
A tremendous exercise in irresponsibility, it is big and clever, by virtue of the fact that it was put together by qualified engineers. Contact your inner child by following the step-by-step instructions for constructing a spud gun that fires faster than the speed of sound, and then obliterating water melons. If this isn't apocalyptic enough, learn how to make aerosols as explosive as A-bombs.

Bored at work?

What better way to while away a few hours at work than indulge in a bit of creative web browsing?

The All-New 'Don't Laugh at   **www.armory.com/**
My Score' Purity Test   **tests/virgin.html**
For the sexually clueless who generally score over 80 per cent on some of the purity tests currently floating around the web. This is a version to help the whiter-than-white to feel better about themselves when all their friends laughed at their original scores.

Ask Jesus   http://askjesus.org
A sacrilegious take on the famous Ask Jeeves site. Simply ask Jesus a
question for a messianic answer or for him to Jesusify a web page
for you.

Battlemail   www.battlemail.com
Fight fierce, manly battles with your friends, via email. Pick a
character, set the moves and see how it fares against your new
enemies.

Build a Rock Star   www.buildarockstar.com
Be Spike Jonze for a while by directing your own rock videos. Could
be waiting a while for the groupies, though.

Bunny Grenade   www.bunnygrenade.com
After seal clubbing, blow up a bunny. No real cruelty involved, just
loads of silly games including 'Stupid Pigeons', 'Parrots In Bars' and
'Bacon Bits'.

Celebrity Spank   www.defused.com/stuff/spank.html
Forever in your face, and there's nothing to be done about it.
Celebrity Spank offers soothing retribution to smug, self-satisfied
and downright annoying 'stars'. Dole out a good slapping and the
world becomes a better place, as the delivery of a good whopping
to Anna Kournikova and Britney Spears will testify.

Centre For the Easily Amused   www.amused.com
Claims to be the ultimate guide to wasting time online. Pointless
activities include sending a virtual milkshake and playing 'Who
Wants To Murder A Millionaire?' Best of all is the fart waffle, a new
way to make music.

Cow Bingo   www4.torget.se/users/p/pudding/fun.html
Syrup topped gold-lamé-clad bingo masters are a thing of the past.
They've been superceded by free-ranging bovines vagueing around a
grid and leaving deposits on the lucky squares. If lottery numbers
were chosen like this, it might be some consolation for the unhappy

millions watching their hard-earned cash slipping into the pockets of Camelot execs.

Death Row　　　　　　www.editionnine.deathrowbook.com/
Serial Killer Quiz　　　　　　noflash/nf_sertest.htm

Assess your chances of ending up zapped in the electric chair or banged up for life. Just calling Mum on Mother's Day doesn't mean that you're such a good person that you'll never end up murdering the neighbourhood kids and keeping their heads in the fridge.

Deck the Halls –　　　　http://losangeles.digitalcity.com/
Beat Up　　　　　　animation/gallery/PlugGame/
Santa　　　　　　　　xmas/deck.htm

Still raises a chuckle even in the midst of a heat wave. This is payback time for a degenerate who likes nothing more than to hang around department stores with small children perched on his lap. Choose your weapon and give the fat fella the thrashing of a lifetime.

Demotivate　　　　　　www.demotivate.com

Life sucks, give it up. A collection of slacker goodies to keep people firmly glued to the sofa.

Down　　　　　　　　http://members.aol.com/
the Pub　　　　　　downthepub/home.htm

Thousands of man hours must be wasted by day dreamers wishing they were down at their local. Now, being at work doesn't mean that you have to miss out completely. A 'virtual pub' with iffy jukebox, bad jokes and silly drinking games – just like a proper boozer.

Emotion Eric　　　　　　www.emotioneric.com

Request an emotion, and Eric will try to act it out for you. Eric is in no danger of a phone call from the Oscars in the foreseeable future.

Halfbakery www.halfbakery.com

A rubbish heap for crazy ideas. Simply upload ridiculous thoughts to join the likes of virtual cemetery flowers, dandelion-eating rabbits, artificial guitar calluses and helicopters with ejector seats.

Have Your Decisions http://thenewage.com/
Made For You oracles

Plenty of ambiguous answers to all of life's problems. Simply ask the question and receive an answer that will allow you to do what you were going to do all along without having to worry that you've done the wrong thing.

How To Decode www.lascofittings.com/
a Bar Code BarCode-EDI/Decode.htm

Unlock the mysteries of those parallel lines. If you happen to be a cash register or scanner, the centre of your universe is Dayton, Ohio – home of the Uniform Code Council. And they want to help you understand their message.

I hate you www.theyrehere.com/ihateyou/ihateyou.html

A particularly vicious page of abuse constructed specifically to send to people you hate.

Lenny Loosejocks' http://shockrave.
Cane Toad Explode macromedia.com

Harmless amphibians are the latest imported Australian wildlife problem. A former staple of cash-strapped hippies who took to licking them for their hallucinogenic secretions, they are now an object of derision of bored Antipodean delinquents, who delight in making them go pop by driving over them in combis. Join Lenny and his trusty dog Donga obliterating them on behalf of the Queensland government for a pittance of beer money.

Madhouse   www.startext.net/homes/
Staring Contest   chris1/staring.htm

Instant annoyance awaits contestants who are greeted with the blank stares from the likes of Homer Simpson and Eric Cartman. Accept it: they're unbeatable.

Name   www.sci.mus.mn.us/sln/tf/c/
That Candybar   crosssection/namethatbar.html

Taxpayers' hard-earned money being squandered in an inspiring way by the Minnesota Science Museum. If you really can't think of anything better to do, identify the chocolate bar from the strange-looking cross-section pictures .

100 Monkeys Search For Intelligent
Monkeys on the Internet   www.100monkeys.org

Inspired by the Search for Extraterrestrial Intelligence, the idea behind 100 Monkeys is to harness the unused processing power of personal computers around the world, or more accurately the collective brainpower of bored employees. Also based on that old adage about monkeys and typewriters eventually coming up with the words of Shakespeare. Just visit the site often.

Punch Captain Kirk   www.well.com/user/vanya/kirk.html

Just watch his syrup go into orbit. William Shatner is rumoured to be one of the least fan-friendly celebs. This site is just for all those Trekkies who've received the Shat brush-off.

Rearrange Fridge Magnets   www.savetz.com/fridge

Arrange them into obscenities on your computer screen if you can't make it to your kitchen.

Sell Your Soul Online   www.nwdc.com/~demona/soul.htm

It's a truly sad state of affairs when people can't find the time to damn themselves for all eternity, but now it's possible to do it online. The Prince of Darkness himself talks you through the three simple steps needed to kiss your soul goodbye.

Sissy Fight 2000 **www.sissyfight.com**
This is an intense war between a bunch of girls who are all out to ruin each other's popularity and self-esteem. Unlike real life, this is played on a computer screen. The object is to physically attack and insult your enemies until they are totally mortified beyond belief. The problem is you have to be careful who you do it to or they'll do the same back to you.

The Spark **www.thespark.com**
A bit like stumbling on a treasure chest of games, The Spark is a veritable online activity set. Its now famous tests (sex, wealth, purity etc.) are becoming legendary and literally millions of people have taken them. They're now branching out to other interesting nonsense, such as giving instructions on how to lose a fight so that the other guy goes to jail, and proven ways to prevent sex. Lose hours of your life here.

Synge **http://synge.com**
For passive-aggressive types with a lot to get off their chests, the Insulter can help. It's a confidential email system that will allow an anonymous message to be delivered while permitting you, the sender, to keep up the pretence of a good relationship and vent your anger without consequence. It even writes the insults if you can't think of any.

Top 10 **www.davesite.com/humor/**
Stupidest Lists **top10/000.shtml**
One man's ongoing battle with boredom. He's created some gems, including things to do with a glass of water, a burned-out light bulb and a brick and different ways to answer the phone.

Totally Useless Office Skills **www.jlc.net/~useless**
Such a great idea that it's spawned a book. Including plenty of tips like how to make telephone music. For clock watchers the world over.

Turn Into
a Cabbage

www.geocities.com/
Heartland/Plains/2144

The author of this site asks the question: how many times have you stared mournfully into the coleslaw and thought to yourself, Gee, I wish I was a cabbage? Well none, but it sure would be interesting to know how many times you have. His cabbage creator will instantly transform you into any number of types of cabbage, a cauliflower or even a Brussels sprout.

The Urinal Game   www.clevermedia.com/arcade/urinal.html

It's important for all tourists trying to blend seamlessly into a deeply repressed Western society to master toilet etiquette. Choosing the correct amenity in some British boozers is not so much desirable but downright essential, as a simple mistake can have fatal consequences. This simple game will provide potentially life-saving advice.

Virtual Dog Shit Creator   www.chocodog.com/vdsc/form.html

Now that street cleaners are getting fairly adept at eradicating any traces of Fido's lunch there is obviously a group of people who are starting to miss playing pavement lottery in their new Nikes. Craft dog turds to exact specifications, consistency, density, dimensions and impact height – or just spend a few days in Paris.

The Virtual
Vomit Page

www.fortunecity.com/meltingpot/
redriver/415/sick.html

Blow chunks without all the smelly cleaning up afterwards. Simply select a location, your stomach contents and – hey presto! – spew your best.

Wacky Advice   http://wackyadvice.com

Exactly as it sounds. If you've got a problem and no one else can help, then it's pretty well guaranteed that it's not going to get any better after seeking advice from this in-house team.

Whack-A-Beaver www.cs.orst.edu/~gottfrhe/
java/whackABeaver.html

Don't expect this little gem in this year's Christmas offering from PlayStation. Virtual animal cruelty has never been so much fun.

What Does Your Phone Number Spell? www.phonespell.org

Nearly every office in the US is armed with net access, supposedly to facilitate the flow of global commerce. In reality it's just providing bored workers with entertainment. If you've got the time or inclination to check this out then you should probably channel your energies into looking for a more fulfilling job.

Out and about

Once you're freed from the PC there's still plenty of amusing things to try, courtesy of these little gems.

The Guys vs. The Girls Burping Contest! http://burpcontest.com

Guys or girls, who really can burp better? This is a repository of belching audio files for the puerile-minded individuals who find this sort of thing funny.

How To Drive http://members.aol.com/
Like a Moron doggiesnot

As if most people actually needed help. If you feel your driving skills are too good and you're nowhere near enough of a liability on the road, brush up your ineptitude here.

Leisure Suit http://desires.com/1.4/
Convention Style/Docs/leisure.html

In case you've been unfortunate enough to miss it there's an annual Leisure Suit Convention held in Des Moines, Iowa, on April Fools' Day. One dedicated veteran says, 'When you put on a leisure suit, it changes your personality.' From tragedy to Travolta with the aid of some electrifying nylon monstrosities.

The Nose Page   www.well.com/user/cynsa/nosepage.html
How many beans can you get up your hooter? This is the place for detailed instructions.

The Official Rock Paper Scissors
Strategy Guide   www.worldrps.com
Memories of interminable childhood car journeys come flooding back at the thought of a few hours of Roshambo. Had the Official Rock Paper Scissors Strategy Guide been around all those years ago, victory would have been assured. What's forgotten is that a sharp rap over the knuckle was always the best way to win.

Santarchy   www.santarchy.com
Yuletide pranks with the cacophonist Santas. Loads of poorly dressed Santas upset the rich shoppers with their doglike howling. Recent police reports following arrests in San Francisco actually state that they were behaving in a decidedly 'Un-Christmas-like fashion'.

The Shotgun Rules Homepage   www.theshotgunrules.com
'Shotgun' as in 'passenger seat of a car', not 'weapon of cowboys and bank robbers'. If you're not the driver, then the best seat in your motor is the one next to them. This site will help make sure that you never have to sit in the back again.

Upper West Side Manhattan Chinese   www.novia.net/~matt/
Restaurant Name Generator   chinese/restaurant.html
Somebody's noticed that there's not a lot of imagination going into naming Chinese restaurants at the moment. For any budding chefs being held back by lack of imagination, this site will have you on the phone to the sign writer within minutes.

31//WACKO OR VISIONARY?

People considered too strange by mainstream society are not always mad. History is riddled with stories of artists and inventors, derided by their peers, eventually dying in obscurity, who are now celebrated as geniuses. The web is a global soapbox for people with oddball theories and new visions of the world to preach their message and swap ideas.

The best information on bizarre phenomena, the paranormal, UFOs, alien abductions, conspiracy theories, mysticism and ghost watching isn't sitting in your local bookshop: it's just a mouse click away.

Aleena's Close Encounters www.geocities.com/Area51/Lair/7180
Ever woken up upside down in bed? Ever had the feeling 'something' has happened but no memory of little green men? Got a splitting headache? Yup, there's plenty of people out there trying to explain their hangovers on alien abduction, Aleena Diamond of Las Vegas being one of them. She's going to help us to spot the telltale signs of being kidnapped by little green men.

Aliens Are Abducting www.sock-monkey.com/
Our Pants pants.html
The owner of this site is of the opinion that the universe is in crisis. He knows it and the aliens know it and he wants to warn the world. Aliens apparently are stealing our pants because of panic and anxiety and when we find ourselves missing in the smalls department our logical minds block out the truth. Scary and mad, but what if he's right?

Altered States of Consciousness Centre www.ascc.org
Nothing to do with Timothy Leary and the tie-dye brigade, but something a bit more spooky. Stories and guidance for those on a

'spiritual journey', so anyone who's had an out of body experience, a lucid dream or an astral projection will be in good company here.

Animals Talk   www.lovepsychics.com/Animalstalk/menu.htm
'Isn't he clever? He knows exactly what you're saying to him.' Everyone's heard proud pet owners mutter this at some point. But loony Art Mayers is convinced that Fido and Tiddles are actually talking back to us through psychic links. He generously explains his theories for us to laugh at.

The Belgrave   www.leicestermercury.co.uk/
Ghost   belgrave-ghost
A ghost sighting actually captured on film. Two ghostly apparitions were filmed wandering through the grounds of Leicester's Belgrave Hall. Read all about the incident and watch the footage before deciding whether it's all a load of rubbish or not.

Conspire.com   www.conspire.com
If you think that everyone's out to get you and the only way that you can stop the secret service listening to your thoughts is to wear a foil hat, you're completely right. They are out to get you and if you want more fuel for your fire come here and you'll truly understand why.

Coverage of the   www.aracnet.com/~atheism/
Inevitable Apocalypse   tocapox4.htm
A collection of stories about wackos to make anyone despair at the state of the world.

Dear SwamiDog   www.swamidog.com
Barking mad or barking psychic? The ambassadors of the paranormal are always going to have a tough time convincing nonbelievers. It's a whole lot worse when you're a miniature schnauzer from Tulsa, Oklahoma. SwamiDog will make online psychic readings and dream interpretations to folk brave enough to email her with a problem.

Dream Oracle   **www.dreamthemes.force9.co.uk**
Dreams have always fascinated people. They stretch from blissful to horrific and, if you can actually remember them on waking, then they don't make any sense. The Dream Oracle is dedicated to finding out what they're all about, which allows dreamers to submit their own and take part in research about dream interpretation.

Farsight Homes   **www.farsight.org**
Scientific Remote Viewing is when trained 'psychics' claim to be able to 'see' events and places many thousands of miles away. US Military Intelligence, the oxymoronic outfit probably responsible for the recent friendly-fire incidents, used them to spy on the Russians.

Fortean Picture Library   **www.forteanpix.demon.co.uk**
Huge collection of pictures of those weird things that people get all excited about seeing. Ghosts, crop circles, abominable snowmen, UFOs, freaks, Nessie, fairies, dwarves, werewolves and other weird phenomena from the real X Files – the archives of the North Wales stock photo library.

**International Association for
Near-Death Studies**   **www.iands.org**
'There was a golden kind of light, brighter than the Sun,' claims Bill, whose brush with the afterlife is one of many documented by the association devoted to greater understanding of near-death experiences. Anyone who's ever been fascinated by *Flat Liners* will get some great follow-up reading here.

International Trepanation Advocacy Group   **www.trepan.com**
One group of people who wouldn't take too kindly to the obvious joke about needing this like a hole in the head. Cavemen thought that headaches and other maladies were caused by a build-up of pressure within the skull and that they could release it through a hole that they would carefully chisel. Medical science has thankfully moved on some distance since these monkeys used to sit around

boring into one another's skull, but not ITAG, who want to tell the world that they're not headcases after all.

Interval Signals   **www.intervalsignals.com**
Radio clips and jingles from stations around the world. Anyone who thinks their local radio station has descended to cheap and cheesy depths ain't heard nothing yet. Catch Angola's Voice of the Resistance of the Black Cockerel and other assorted delights.

The Knights of Probity   **www.carenduna.freeuk.com**
In the post-feminist world a bit of chivalry is frowned upon and 'true gentlemen' are heading for a knee in the crotch. Step forth Cir Aelfric deRochefort, Grand Commander of the Knights of Probity, who will help people with their 'personal honour code' and show them how to live their lives like people did in the good old days.

The LeyHunter   **www.leyhunter.com/**
Journal   **leyhunt/welcome.html**
Eighty years ago somebody noticed that churches, prehistoric sites, stone circles and hill forts often occurred along dead-straight lines. What could this mean? Lots of strange theories about the fact that it was no accident and they were all built along ley lines, which increased their power.

The Loch Ness Monster
Research Society   **www.ness-monster.com**
With the 'world's largest database of Nessie-related information', the LNMRS take the hunt for the monster seriously. No mention of the fact that it's only ever seen by drunks, staggering home from the pub. You can also see those inevitable photos that look like a load of old tyres floating about.

The Psychedelic Shack   **http://homepages.tcp.co.uk/~natalie**
Natalie is a 'transgendered' person, who just happened to be born a bloke, and wants to help others in her situation. Her partner and

soul mate, Karen, also gets a look-in and they explain how they've brought up their two kids, Andrew and Aaron.

Reverse Speech   www.reversespeech.com

This must have been where all that kerfuffle about playing heavy-metal records backwards started. David John Oates believes that when he listens to tapes of people played backwards he discovers their 'deepest regions of the consciousness'. The site allows people to listen to famous audio clips so that they can find out whether they need to go on one of Mr Oates's, presumably expensive, courses.

Strange Magazine   www.strangemag.com

Bizarre collection of tales, myths and other stories from people with overactive imaginations from around the world. Find out all about the Wisconsin Werewolf, mermaids and extraterrestrial abductions in this online edition of the bi-annual US magazine.

Ultimate   http://ourworld.compuserve.com/
Ufologists   homepages/AndyPage

'I Think We're Alone Now' is just one song that won't be playing at this lot's Christmas party. Photos, famous UFOs, a Who's Who of ufology, theories, personal sightings and the latest UFO gossip. For those who took *Close Encounters* a little too seriously.

32//WEBCAMS

Webcams are proliferating, as the public's appetite for voyeurism remains unassuaged. Offering constantly updated images accessible from computers the world over, they have the potential to offer virtual visits to the most bewildering scenarios. It all started as a bit of a joke when the inventors of this innocuous piece of technology pointed a working cam at the coffee pot in their staff room. Cams now snoop on everything from the mind-numbingly mundane to the off-the-wall weird. Its *tour de force* was the first live Internet birth in 1999, but there are plenty of remarkable views still out there.

Cockney Pavement Terror   www.backfire.co.uk
Which isn't thousands of irate Millwall fans, but a disturbed delivery man who set up a spy camera in his van. Urban voyeurism taken to new levels of tedium, which will hopefully be outlawed by new privacy laws.

Colchester Web Cam   www.actual.co.uk/streetcam.html
Splashed over Saturday broadsheets in 1999 was the story of the Neuhoff family, who moved from a hick town in New Mexico to this one in Essex, lured by the beauty of images from this street cam.

Cow &   www.euronet.nl/users/idi_rad1/
Chicken   cow-and-chicken/cowcam.html
A less than tasteful glimpse of commercial meat farming. New Jersey Neanderthals can enjoy the sight of their next fajita before it's placed on their dinner table in front of them.

Fridge Cam   www.electrolux.com/node230.asp
An employee of a well-known Swedish domestic-appliance manufacturer has set up the Fridge Cam in his own coldbox. At any time of the day or night it's possible to check out the eating habits of a mildly dysfunctional (or should that read boring?) Stockholm family. On the plus side it's possible to email Daddy Tom when the

milk supply runs low, so that he can show Mummy Pirkko what a fantastic 21st-Century man he is by picking up a few pints on the way back from work.

Ghost   www.flyvision.org/sitelite/
Watcher   Houston/GhostWatcher
Installing webcams the length and breadth of your home (including under the bed) to convince an uninterested world that it's haunted means you're probably in the wrong kind of home.

The Live Lobster Cam   www.midcoast.com/lobcam
Crustacean entrapment live from a 'regulation' lobster trap dunked into the sea somewhere off the coast of New England. More of an exercise in scamming some free computer equipment than an advancement in scientific knowledge.

Ministry of Sound   www.ministryofsound.co.uk
Chuck Berry found himself in serious schtuck when he tried it, but anything goes on the net. This bastion of British club culture has installed a cam in the women's toilet. Admittedly it's aimed at the mirrors by the basins, not poking through the walls into one of the cubicles.

Nipple Server   www.spinnwebe.com/nipple
A baffling daily update on the state of the webmaster's left nipple. In a world rife with poverty and hatred this is a strange use of technology. Visitors are even asked to assess said appendage for colour, perkiness, panache and overall nipplish quality.

The Presidential Trash Can   www.trashcam.com
Claiming to allow visitors an insight into President Bill's trashcan but looks suspiciously like a window. A quick glance at the daily papers suggests that the filthiest piece of garbage in the White House is situated between its famous resident's lug holes.

Severe Tyre Damage http://chocolate.research.digital.com
STD to their friends (geddit?) claim to be the web's first live band.
Allowing the public to 'drop in' on their rehearsals has ensured their
total lack of success in today's music scene.

Ski Resorts www.rsn.com/cams/copper
Hardly a coincidence that it's always snowing in ski resorts with web
cams. It doesn't take the brain of Einstein to realise that pointing a
snow cannon at the lens is going to pull in the tourist dollar.

Sleep www.sleepstation.com
An online slumber party. Lots of webcams of sleeping people.

Steve's Ant Farm www.stevesantfarm.com
Marvel as a million full stops go about their daily business of making
tunnels and performing Herculean feats with their next meal.

Web Cam World www.webcamworld.com
For further webcam delights check back often. This is the central
repository.

Yellow Wood Llamas http://ywl.com/webcam.htm
The daily goings-on of a commercial llama farm, where one of
Bolivia's lesser-known exports can be seen browsing the verdant
pastures of Indiana. The biggest revelation to most is the very
existence of such places.

33//WEB CELEBRITIES

Back in the dark old days when the web was a small, friendly community based around sharing free information, news of humorous websites spread like wildfire. They generally weren't that funny but spun off endless themed imitations. Soon, these sites became web celebrities in their own rights. Then some bright spark invented the idea of webrings, which allow similar sites to link to each other.

The first web crazes were really the magic eight balls and the 'Ate My Balls' series, then somehow Mr T got in on the act. By this point, office email was a major force in the global dissemination of jokes and humorous sites started popping up everywhere. About once a year something so bizarre pops up that the whole web audience is captivated and news even manages to break beyond the confines of cyberspace into the outside world. Recently, a Turkish man became the victim of a practical joke that rocketed him to global celebrity status. The world eagerly awaits the birth of the next web celebrity.

Magic 8 ball

Those tacky pool-ball toys that seem to return endless ambiguous answers to any questions made a smooth transition to the web, spawning endless copies of the originals. Every web celebrity has its own magic 8 ball, Mahir, Mr T, even dead rock stars. A good way to start is to drill through the Yahoo directory or simply type in:
http://dir.yahoo.com/Entertainment/Humor/Advice/
Web_Oracles/Eight_Ball

Kurt Cobain's Magic Talking 8 Ball   www.xworld.com/cobain
The dead grunge god can still reach out and touch your desperate life.

Ate my balls

Originally American slang for being on somebody's case, the 'Ate My Balls' websites started popping up with balls being eaten all over the place. Legend states that it all started with the legendary Mr T, but we'll probably never know. In fact, if you're a celebrity and you're not eating someone's balls then your career is on a fast track downhill. There are hundreds of these sites, all basically the same and all linked by various webrings. Good starting points are:

Ate My Balls Webring	**www.geocities.com/SiliconValley/Pines/3640/ring.html**
Krazy Keith's (almost complete) Ate My Balls linx page	**http://members.tripod.com/~krazy_keith/Ballz.html**

Mr T

Mr T, the bizarrely dressed, gold-clad muscle factor in the A-Team, never really had the momentous acting career he probably hoped for. His fame, though, seems to be assured with the hundreds of websites that are dedicated to or at least feature him. Most of them seem to have come to life after a thousand drunken conversations that probably started with 'Who do you reckon is harder – Mr T or XXX?' There are so many Mr T vs. (insert celebrity, planet, corporation here) sites that even search engines have trouble listing them. There's only one rule: Mr T always wins.

Of course, as soon as there's a new web phenomenon, Mr T will rear his ugly head in some form or other.

Dancin' Mr T   **www.din.or.jp/~cotta/dance.html**
Getting in on the act.

Mr T Ate My Balls   **www.geocities.com/nkpatel/mrt**
And nobody would want that.

Mr T vs.   **www.sit.wisc.edu/**
Everything   **~kljense3/MrTvs.html**
The Mr T portal, with links to all his conflicts.

The T'inator   **http://firefly.sparse.org/~mrt/**
Think your web page is tough? Not as tough as it could have been if Mr T had written it. Simply submit the URL for the muscle treatment, you crazy fools.

Dancing things

Once upon a time somebody made a crude animated GIF of a hamster moving about. It was put on a web page and then an identical one was put next to it until there was a whole row of them. Another hamster image was made and another row constructed. The same thing happened over and over until the whole browser page was full of jerkily moving rodents.

Nothing remarkable at all about that until the bright spark who made the page decided to embed some audio. You know the worst chart songs that you hear in a shop that linger in your brain for the rest of the day? Well the audio track that was attached to the Hamsterdance page was hundreds of times more infectious and could possibly be the most nauseatingly cheerful little ditty ever composed.

This page then made the rounds on the office email circuit, where its popularity spread like wildfire. The song would start up in a staggered fashion from one desk and then spread around the office as people opened their emails.

This captured the public imagination to the point that web developers fell over themselves to make variations on the theme, the worst culprits of which include 657 links to 'Dance' sites on the webring. And here are just a few.

Alien Dance	www.aliendance.com
Alternadance	http://members.tripod.com/ proteinmonkees/Alternadance/altdance.html
Armadillo Dance	www.armadillodance.com
Cheesecake dance	http://members.xoom.com/Beefstupid/ cheesecakedance.htm
Cow Dance	www.cowdance.com
Dance In Our Pants	www.amused.com/links/dance.php3
Dancing hamsters	www.dancinghamsters.com
The Dancing Baby Dance Club	www.dbaby.com
The Dancing Baby Page	http://dancing-baby.net
Dr Who Dance	http://rtf.kracked.com/drwho
Fishy Dance	www.fishydance.com
Funky Pez Dance Of Love	http://millennium.fortunecity.com/ lilac/403/pezdance.html
Hamsterdance	www.hamsterdance.com
Herve Villechaize Dance	http://tradedforwheat.com/ meshugenah/dancingherve.html
Infectious Organism Dance	www.angelfire.com/ga/ scantsanity/amoeba.html
Lawyer Dance	www.lawyerdance.com
Leprechaun Dance	www.leprechaundance.com
Lizard Dance	www.lizarddance.com
Media Bore Dance	www.enteract.com/~campers/Media
Pikachu Dance	www.pikachudance.com

Prince Charles Dance	www.strutyourfunkystuff.com/ charles-dance.html
Stick Man Dance	www.stickmandance.com
The FatGuy Dance!	www.amused.com/fatguydance.html
Turtle Dance	www.turtledance.com

Newgrounds

*The brainchild (on **www.newgrounds.com**) of Tom Fulp, who started it when he was a mere seventeen years old. No website has so consistently pushed back the boundaries of good taste like Newgrounds. Putting a particularly nasty spin on modern populist culture, its highlights include:*

Assassin   www.newgrounds.com/assassin
You know you've hit a social nerve when national newspapers jump on the story about a charity up in arms about a website. Not that the website was advocating paedophilia or serial killing or anything like that, but Scots People Against Child Abuse got themselves into a right tizz about Assassin, a cute little game that allows irksome celebrities to meet their maker in a fitting fashion: dropping the *Titanic* on Leonardo di Caprio or crashing Britney Spears in her monster truck or wiping out the Power Rangers with a 1,000-ton mega-robot.

Beep Me Jesus   www.newgrounds.com/beeper
Ok, it's simple … Say your question out loud so God can hear it, or concentrate really hard on your question and he will read your mind. God relays his response to Jesus, who then relays it to the beeper! Push the button and hey presto – you have the answers to life's mysteries!

Club a Seal   www.newgrounds.com/seals

The perpetrator of this one is an avowed animal lover, so the Club a Seal game was originally designed with heavy irony. The humourless animal-rights activists who stumbled across it failed to see the funny side and emailed their protests in droves.

Mahir Cagri

The Original Mahir   http://members.xoom.com/
page   _XOOM/primall/mahir

Mahir was a perfectly normal Turkish guy whose hobbies included swimming, table tennis and playing the guitar. The day one of his friends put together a web page in his honour, featuring a few photos of Mahir indulging in some of his hobbies, he unwittingly became the web's biggest celebrity. According to him, somebody stole his web page and changed it slightly to include the phrase 'I like sex and I kiss you'. That's when the whole thing went bananas: his web hosting company's servers crashed, he was deluged with phone calls and just about every newspaper printed features about this reluctant hero. It all culminated in a tour of the US sponsored by an online travel agent, and Mahir wore a permanently perplexed look on his face. He now proudly advertises web companies for a living.

The Sequel   www.kissmahir.com

The official Mahir webring includes 58 spin-off parody sites, including a 'Mahir Dance' and 'Mahir Ate My Balls', all easily found by visiting the original site. His place in the annals of web history is assured.

And finally . . .

Celebrity Death Slalom   westword.com/extra/cds

Remember when drunken American celebrities were popping off by the shipload after terminal accidents with trees on skiing trips?

The crew responsible for this site don't think that the death count should stop at the Sonny Bonos of the world and that Leonardo Di Caprio, Calista Flockhart, Howard Stern, the Spice Girls and Jerry Springer should get the tree treatment too.

David Hasselhoff is the AntiChrist www.esquilax.com/baywatch/index.shtml

A man with no apparent star qualities who is immensely rich and spends his life surrounded by some of the world's most beautiful women. How can it be? Maybe the fact that he's a household name in Germany is the first clue, but one look at this site should be enough to convince even the hardest sceptic that Mr Knight Rider is in fact the devil. From his rising out of the sea to his dual antennae, there can be no doubt that he is evil to the core.

The Manson Gossip Hell Message Board http://members.boardhost.com/mansongossip

Marilyn Manson is a curious phenomenon. Anyone listening to America's moral majority would think that he was the tool of Satan, sent to Earth to destroy the minds of the nation's youth. In reality, he's having a great time wearing silly clothes and the only person who seems to get the joke is him, as the postings on this fan message board will testify.

Pamela Des Barres http://electricgypsy.com/pamela

The *über*-groupie Pam hawks her talents in cyberspace. Buy the books or just chat online with her.

The Really Big Button That Doesn't Do Anything www.pixelscapes.com/spatulacity/button.htm

A slightly surreal experience. Pages all over the web feature a solitary button (usually red) that invites you to push it. When you do, nothing happens. That's it, thousands have tried, nobody's revealed anything useful.

34//EPILOGUE

So there we are, then, after our brief tour around some of the more interesting oddities cluttering up the web. The Internet, and more specifically the web, is a completely different beast from the nerdy little collection of grey pages that were around five or six years ago. Since then it's become a brain dump for the population's thoughts. As we've seen, if you want to know about something, anything, there's a web page out there with your name on it.

Where are we now?
Is the culture of the web any different now from the pioneering days of HTML? Yes and no. Those cybernauts who pushed back the frontiers of human communication are still there – they're just hugely outnumbered by lumbering corporations who have been caught unawares by the information revolution and opportunistic web entrepreneurs out to make a fast buck and get their cheesy grin flashed about the world's press.

In those early days it was geek currency to have your own website. Didn't matter what you put on it: just thrusting your stake in the ground was enough. It showed you were part of the strange, evangelising digerati, who knew something that the rest of the world didn't. No way was this ever going to be the CB radio of the nineties. We've seen the stupidest ideas ever to emerge from someone's mouth becoming a cheap cyber laugh and others mushrooming into massive companies.

Nowadays, just having your own website quietly hosted on your college server doesn't really cut the mustard. It's getting harder and harder to find college websites that are anything but formulaic rites of passage for their authors. The bizarre is getting harder to find. In fact, just having your own daft site merely shows a lack of ambition. The college geeks who made all these daft little sites are now web designers living out their wacky dreams with corporations falling over themselves to get their hands on them. Strutting around with their Palm Pilots and BMX bikes, recognisable by their hip urban look, they've changed the working environment by holding old duffers in management to ransom with their overinflated salaries.

You're a bit odd if you want to have a wacky site today and you haven't got a twenty-page business plan that will take your drunken pub moment across multiple emerging digital platforms from shiny offices all over the world. The commercial world has embraced the web and tried to claim it for its own. The wacky idea that would once have given your friends a laugh is now your closely guarded road to infinite stock riches, as long as you find that venture capitalist who'll give you the money to make it happen.

What's making things even more difficult is that publishing a website isn't even that easy any more. In the early days anyone who could operate a toaster could probably put a page of text and photos up on a website. Today it's all about databases, information architecture, rich media content and emerging platforms. Basically the cunning little mammal that was the web is now an unwieldy, lumbering monster with production processes that would give a rocket-launch program a run for its money.

Is the content out there any better? Sure, there's the fastest 24-hour news on demand, a company that will deliver you toothpaste from Greenland and sports results that you never knew you needed. But the most interesting thoughts are always the ones from the left field. In our postmodern society the underground has been dragged into daylight and is scrabbling to return because it doesn't like what it's seen. Special-interest groups found the web a joy for meeting like-minded people and are now inundated with abuse from cheeky little eight-year-olds with their parents' credit cards.

Stories abound that encapsulate the American dream. Loads of websites out there started out as quirky little ideas that captured the public imagination and snowballed. If you're enthusiastic about your stuff then you can compete with the best journalists in print on equal terms. No arduous journalistic training and years making the tea for some high and mighty celebrity writer. Just give up the day job, work every hour of the day on a constant diet of hamburgers and fizzy drinks and someone might just come along and offer you enough money to turn your hobby into your first business.

The comfortable expense-lunch culture of the media has been grabbed by the throat and shaken hard. It's trying to regain a bit of control after being caught badly on the hop. When AOL, ten years ago an upstart Internet company, bought Time Warner, the world's biggest media company, the resultant mega-corporation had a greater cash flow than Russia. The rule books have been rewritten.

The future
It's out there somewhere. Has the weird website had its day? Possibly, but a good idea is still a good idea and splashing it on to a web page is still the cheapest way to get it out to a lot of people. If comedy websites are just embryonic corporate sell-outs, what does the future hold for the Internet?

Well, people at work are always going to be bored. Now that companies see PCs as being as essential for the smooth running of an office as a plentiful supply of biros, there are going to be more and more people looking for something to tickle their fancy when they know that they should be knuckling down.

Emerging technologies may be the key. Already in Japan there's more Internet access through mobile phones than desktop PCs. WAP phones and their successors will allow people to browse their favourite sites while communicating with each other. We've all seen how people at bus stops would rather chat to their friends on their mobiles than stand vacantly watching tramps shambling down the road. It's human nature to want to be stimulated in some form or another, and combining people's insatiable appetite for mobile phones with the Internet should make for interesting watching.

The desk-bound Internet itself is going to start changing soon. Clunky old websites that freeze when the merest hint of video comes down the wires should soon be a thing of the past. Broadband websites will allow near-broadcast-quality video delivery. Why should we care?

The creator of *Ren & Stimpy* was turfed out of his job for pushing back the boundaries of what was deemed tasteful for young kids. Undeterred, he decided that his art should be pumped out through his website. Slightly hampered by technology and lack of cash, it wasn't the greatest success. Now things are going to be different: there's just not enough decent content to fill up the outlets available. With TV-quality broadcast for Internet prices a whole generation of filmmakers, documentary makers and animators are going to be able to push the boundaries of their art free from the constraints of TV execs losing sleep from the threat of potential advertisers pulling their money away. The dreaded layer of middle management may have had its day and interesting times are just around the corner. TV scheduling is going to become a thing of the past as people get to watch what they want to watch when they want to watch it.

Where now?
The last ten years have seen some of the greatest ever changes in communication. The human condition is both blessed and cursed with an insatiable desire to communicate. That's what got us out of the trees in the first place. The explosive growth of the Internet is just fuelling people's desire to be heard. The boundaries between TVs, PCs and phones will blur to a distant memory as technologies

converge, and still we're going to want great ideas to pump out of the resulting products, whatever they are.

As for the present, there are still plenty of daft ideas being pumped out on to the web. Instead of being badly coded grey pages they're slick ezines being run by sixteen-year-old kids with teams of writers and designers.

The ones that have appeared since this book was written can be found simply by going to your favourite search engine and typing in the following words: **bizarre**, **strange**, **weird**, **funny**. Or any daft idea that pops into your head. There's guaranteed to be some joker who got there before you did. If you're really lazy go to Ask Jeeves (**www.ask.com**) and ask him to point you to the kind of weird stuff that you like. Happy hunting.

35//FINDING THE WEIRD

Search Engines are popping up all of the time. This is by no means all of them but it's certainly enough to get started.

UK search engines

AltaVista UK	www.altavista.co.uk
Brit Index	www.yacc.co.ukbritind
CyberSearch UK	www.cybersearch.co.uk
Demon Site of Sites	www.brains.demon.co.uk
Info-Links Launchpad	www.info-links.com/uk
Media UK	www.mediauk.com
UK Directory	www.ukdirectory.com
UK Plus	www.ukplus.com
UK Search	www.uksearch.com
UK Web Library	www.scit.wlv.ac.uk/wwlib
UK Yellow Web Search	www.yell.com
Yahoo in the UK	www.yahoo.co.uk

Web search engines

Alta Vista	www.altavista.com
Disinformation	www.disinfo.com
Docking Bay	www.dockingbay.com
Euroferret	www.muscat.co.uk/euroferret

Excite	www.excite.com
Excite City.net	www.city.net
Eye on the web	www.eyeontheweb.com
G.O.D.	www.god.co.uk
Google	www.google.com
HotBot	www.hotbot.com
InfoSeek Guide	http://guide.infoseek.com
LookSmart	www.looksmart.com
Lycos	www.lycos.com
Magellan	www.mckinley.com
NerdWorld	www.nerdworld.com
NetGuide	www.netguide.com
OneKey	www.onekey.com
OpenText	search.opentext.com
Point	www.pointcom.com
Pointers	www.pointers.co.uk
REX	www.rex.skyline.net
Search.com	www.search.com
Search.Onramp.Net	search.onramp.net
Surfpoint	www.surfpoint.com
TradeWave Galaxy	www.einet.net
Web Wombat	www.webwombat.com.au
WebCrawler	www.webcrawler.com
What U Seek	www.whatuseek.com

| WWWomen | www.wwwomen.com |
| Yahoo | www.yahoo.com |

Metasearchers

All 4 One	http://all4one.com
Ask Jeeves	www.ask.com
Cyber411	www.cyber411.com/search
DigiSearch	www.digiway.com/digisearch
DogPile	www.dogpile.com
Go2Net Search	www.go2net.com/search
Highway 61	www.highway61.com
Inference Find!	www.inference.com/ifind
The Internet Sleuth	www.isleuth.com
iSearch UK	www.isearch.co.uk
Mamma	www.mamma.com
MetaCrawler	metacrawler.cs.washington.edu
MotherLoad	www.cosmix.com/motherload
Prime Search	www.delta.com/prime.com/pssearch.htm
Starting Point	www.stpt.com
Super Search	www.robtex.com/search/query.htm
SuperSeek	www.superseek.com
Web Search	www.web-search.com
Where.com Link Search	where.com/ls/LinkSearch.html

Email, news searchers and people finders

BigFoot	www.bigfoot.com
CataLyst	www.lsoft.comlistslistref.html
DejaNews	www.dejanews.com
Dominis E-zines	www.dominis.com/Zines
E-mag Search	www.etext.org
ESP-Email Search Program	www.esp.co.uk
Forum One	www.forumone.com
Four11	www.four11.com
InfoSpace Internet Address Finder	www.infospace.com
Liszt	www.liszt.com
Populus	www.populus.net
Reference.com	www.reference.com
SwitchBoard	www.switchboard.com
Tile.net	http://tile.net
Usenet Channel	www.UsenetChannel.com
Usenet FAQs	www.cs.ruu.nlcgi-binfaqwais
Who Where?	www.whowhere.com
Who's Who On-line	www.whoswho-online.com

//INDEX

//OTHER GREAT VIRGIN INTERNET GUIDES

The Virgin Guide to the Internet
The advice you need to plug in, log on and get going.

The Virgin Internet Shopping Guide
Great things to buy.

The Virgin Family Internet Guide
Get the best out of the Internet - and lock out the worst.

The Virgin Internet Travel Guide
The complete guide to destinations and deals.

The Virgin Internet Music Guide
The web is alive - with the sound of music.

The Virgin Internet Money Guide
Get your finances sorted online.

The Virgin Internet Business Guide
The essential companion for anyone in business.

The Virgin Internet Auction Guide
Bid for an online bargain.

The Virgin Internet Research Guide
How to find out just about anything on the net.

The Virgin Internet Guide for Kids
Adults - keep out!

For more information, ask your local bookseller - or check out
http://www.virginbooks.com